ADVANCE PRAISE

"In her latest book, *Reclaim Your Life: For Wives at the Crossroads*, attorney, life coach, and bestselling author Aya Fubara Eneli shares insights that speak to the pain many women experience as they reconcile their hopes and their dreams for their marriage with the reality of their lives. While some may advocate divorce or playing the martyr when faced with challenges in a marriage, this book serves as a powerful call to women to go beyond the surface to gain a better understanding of why and how they've arrived at this point in their lives, so they can be equipped to create the life they dream of.

Aya provides practical insights and specific strategies for women to heal and grow by reclaiming their power. This book and specifically the Best Wife Ever Challenge align with the values of Black and Married with Kids and will positively impact every marriage. It is an undeniable truth that this time next year, your marriage and life will either be better or worse based on the choices you make now. Choosing to read this book and apply the principles it covers is a powerful step to stopping the pain in your marriage, so you can live your dreams."

—Ronnie and Lamar Tyler, Founders of Black and Married with Kids

"My friend Aya has done it again—made the impossible possible. Not sure how she does all she does, but it is done with excellence. With 25 years of marriage education under my belt, I am confident this book has the potential to impact America's sad state of marriage. *Reclaim Your Life* is a powerful resource for women…but men and sons will indirectly benefit from these direct, authentic, and compassionate words."

—Dr. Byron Weathersbee, President/Co-Founder of Legacy Family Ministries and Author of *Before Forever* and *To Have and To Hold*

"As a mental health professional and trauma specialist, I have worked with, and continue to work with, many women trying to find ways to reclaim their lives. I have read many books with tools and techniques for women to use as they focus on building or rebuilding their relationships and marriages, not to mention all the resources available to help them learn new ways to examine and strengthen their relationships. So I can definitively say that *Reclaim Your Life: Guidance for Wives at the Crossroads* by Aya Fubara Eneli, Esq., is one of the top 10 books for a healthy marriage that every woman, and man, should read. Moreover, it is an invaluable tool for anyone who works with couples because the structure of the book makes it an effective therapeutic tool.

This book by Aya Fubara Eneli looks at one of the most common problems many women struggle with: navigating the foundation of marriage with all the complexities and intricacies that come with it. The different "emotions," or possible phases of marriage are identified as: divorce, destined for failure, the dream marriage, true desire, self-reflection, creating your ideal, sex and intimacy, eradicating the limits to being a phenomenal wife, scaling hurdles, and the action plan. In each chapter, Aya guides women through their unique needs and thoughts, and how these needs must be met and thoughts must be clarified as we aim to create our ideal marriage. The beauty of the book is that throughout, she uses concrete examples from her own experiences, as well as experiences from women she has coached to illustrate her concepts.

With this book, Aya Fubara Eneli, Esq., is on her way to being one of the most sought-after marriage experts we have. *Reclaim Your Life* is based on 23 years of proven research, her own marriage, and she brilliantly lays out how awareness of dysfunctional relationship patterns can help one stop the cycles, which is an important key to a healthy marriage in the present. This book is simple and direct and works for marriages at any stage. It helps the reader step back and look at their lives and marriage in a practical manner, while offering guidance on which road to take."

—Somiari Demm, MA/MDiv, CTS, CYT

"This is a much-needed book for women everywhere. The author has an authentic, relatable writing style, which gives one more of an incentive to follow through with the author's well-researched and self-tested questions and challenges. In fact, this is more of a life-manual than a book. You will get more out of this book if you approach it as you would a manual or a workbook. Follow through with the recommended exercises and challenge yourself to answer the soul-searching questions. You'll be glad you did. As someone who has seen firsthand the beneficial effects of some of the principles, shared by the author, I encourage women (whether wives or not) to really go through this material and reclaim your life. You owe it to yourself!"

—Sabine Chibueze, Pharmaceutical Executive

Reclaim Your Life is as intense as it is a masterpiece, a go-to resource for self-discovery and restoration within marriage. I could not stop reading till I got to the 10th chapter, very fluid, engaging, and brilliant. I will read it again slowly and get to the action points. I strongly recommend it as a great marriage resource. Five stars!

—Eden Onwuka, Author of *The Power of a Single Story*

RECLAIM
YOUR LIFE
Guidance for Wives at the Crossroads

RECLAIM YOUR LIFE

Guidance for Wives at the Crossroads

Aya Fubara Eneli, Esq.

Foreword by Shannon Ethridge

RECLAIM YOUR LIFE
Published by Purposely Created Publishing Group™
Copyright © 2018 Aya Fubara Eneli

All rights reserved.

Neither the author nor the publisher assumes any responsibility for errors, omissions, or contrary interpretations of the subject matter herein. Any perceived slight of any individual or organization is purely unintentional.

Scriptures marked NIV are taken from the New International Version®. Copyright © 1973, 1978, 1984, 2011 by Biblica, Inc.™. All rights reserved.

Author's photo courtesy of Annie Dockery

Printed in the United States of America

ISBN: 978-1-947054-85-1

Special discounts are available on bulk quantity purchases by book clubs, associations and special interest groups. For details email: sales@publishyourgift.com or call (888) 949-6228.
For information logon to: www.PublishYourGift.com

This book is dedicated to my mother, Her Royal Highness, Alabota Dr. Vinolia Fubara, née Peterside, whose courage and discipline inspire me to embrace hope, face my fears, and choose love in all things.

TABLE OF CONTENTS

FOREWORD

After fifteen years of speaking at conferences and publishing my own books, I have been asked numerous times, "How can I do what you do?" I learned there are many other people on the planet who feel "pregnant" with a message or testimony that God has entrusted to them. Rather than offering a quick pat on the back and a cliché or two about working hard and sticking with it, I decided to develop something that would truly catapult them in the right direction.

In 2009, I created an online mentorship program with twelve lessons to guide those who wanted to establish or enlarge their own speaking or writing platform. I call it the BLAST Mentorship Program, which stands for Building Leaders, Authors, Speakers & Teachers. Since that time, over four hundred individuals have benefited from this material. The book that you're holding in your hands is written by one of those people, and it's my delight to tell you about MY first introduction to Aya as YOUR first introduction to this book.

Two years after launching this program, we held a Class Reunion of sorts, combined with a new video taping of all twelve lessons for those who wanted to fly in four days early to be in the live audience. All of the material covered was originally designed to be digested over a twelve-month span of time, so you can imagine how overloaded people felt at the end of the four-day blitz of a refresher course. They all felt like they'd taken a drink from a fire hydrant, or tried to go surfing in a tsunami.

At the end of those four exhilarating and exhausting days, others flew in for just the "reunion" part of the experience, beginning that Friday night. I had my concerns that I'd packed the schedule way too tight, and that the folks who'd been there all week would be incredibly restless or zoned out for the rest of the weekend, unable to focus on the other, fresher folks who would be speaking and sharing their stories and passions.

The first speaker I had lined up after all that curriculum-video-taping-madness had ceased was Aya Eneli. As we transitioned into a more relaxed reunion mode, I wondered if she would be able to hold everyone's attention . . . to keep their focus . . . to stir something new in them that hadn't already been stirred multiple times throughout the week. I braced myself for the real possibility that she would be faced by a depleted audience that simply had nothing left to give to even just one more speaker. Fortunately, I've never been more incorrect!

Aya took that microphone like a woman on a mission—a God-ordained mission. As she shared some of her incredibly powerful stories about what God had done in her life, marriage, and family, the crowd was absolutely mesmerized! It was like the entire group got their second wind, and were soaring higher spiritually than they had been all week! By the time Aya wrapped up, there wasn't a dry eye in the room. If it had been a big tent revival, I have no doubt every person would have rushed down to the makeshift altar to surrender their lives to the Lord all over again!

Aya brings that same passion, vulnerability, power, authenticity, and eloquence to this book, *Reclaim Your Life: For Wives at the Crossroads.* This book is a must-read, not just for wives who are experiencing challenges in their marriage and are weighing their options, but also as a very useful resource for women contemplating marriage in the first place.

While there are other books on marriage, this book specifically speaks to the hearts of women. It builds on the understanding that no one comes into their marriage as a blank slate. Rather, all our experiences and relationships from birth shape who we are and how we choose our mates, as well as how we act in those relationships.

Aya's background as an attorney, a life coach, and a Christian brings great balance and practical value to this delicate topic. She doesn't assume an overly spiritual tone, a problem that books by Christians can sometimes suffer from. Instead, while Aya grounds the healing of her marriage and its continuing growth on her Christian faith, she also acknowledges the realities and legal ramifications of the choices people must make.

Using her own story, solid research, and vignettes from her coaching clients, Aya gently leads her readers down a path of self-discovery that provides clarity—not just on how to address their current marital challenges, but also on how they arrived at this juncture in the first place. She also unpacks practical ways for women to reclaim their power and create the life they really desire.

This book treats no subject as taboo, going from discussions about sexual intimacy and financial stressors to abuse and even the less-than-honorable motivations that sometimes lead us to seek marriage in the first place. This book encourages us to come clean with ourselves so we can move forward with clarity, confidence, power, and passion.

I have no doubt you're going to be incredibly moved by Aya's stories and teachings as well, so put on your seatbelt and get ready for a wild ride.

Shannon Ethridge, MA
Author of twenty-two books, including the million copy bestseller *Every Woman's Battle* series
www.shannonethridge.com
www.blastmentoring.com

INTRODUCTION

She called me to get some advice on a situation in her workplace that was causing her angst. We walked through her options and she seemed relieved that she now had a clear plan on how to proceed, but I could sense something else was bothering her. I asked, "Shelly, is there anything else you would like to talk about? I have a few minutes."

There was a long pause and then, in a barely audible voice, she whispered, "Please help me. I've tried to do it on my own. My marriage is killing me."

Shelly is a smart and very accomplished woman. When she walks into a room, you can sense her quiet dignity. She isn't one to draw attention to herself, and yet she is well-known and respected in every circle. She has the reputation of being a go-getter, a hard worker, and a woman not afraid to go after her dreams and make the impossible possible. She wears many hats, moving from role to role with ease, and people often marvel at how she does it all. Physically attractive and yet down-to-earth, Shelly wears her self-confidence and drive like an invisible cape. Simply put, she is Wonder Woman personified, easily juggling a very bright professional career with being a mother and wife while still making time to be active in her community.

Shelly is admired by most, intimidating to many, and inspiring to all. All, it seems, but her husband, Timothy.

Timothy showed up as her knight in shining armor. He was good looking, charming, and focused, and well on his way to creating a life few dreamed of. Although she had had her share of suitors, it felt good to be singled out by him. He lavished her with attention, and soon she was dreaming of their life together. She's not quite sure she ever got into the specifics of her dreams with him or even with herself. She just knows that they ended with: ". . . And they lived happily ever after." Her family and friends alike all congratulated her on what a good catch he was. Shelly was on cloud nine.

> ## "I WAS TIRED OF SWALLOWING MY WORDS JUST TO KEEP THE PEACE."

But things don't seem so rosy anymore. Something changed when she hit her forties. In her words: "I just couldn't do it anymore. I was tired of swallowing my words just to keep the peace." Her dream for her marriage seems to have morphed into a nightmare. When she looks at him, instead of seeing her knight, she sees a virtual stranger. She can't remember the last time he complimented her. He complains about her work schedule, refuses to acknowledge her accomplishments, and barely helps out in the home or with the children; when he does help, he seems to expect a parade in his honor. He berates her with his words and seems baffled when she rebuffs his sexual advances. But what's the point of making love when you don't feel love?

Shelly is tired of carrying the burden of keeping the marriage and family together all by herself. She is up early and often works late into the night to keep up with her responsibilities at her job and in her home. She has some new opportunities at work but is hesitant to go after them because of the effect they could have on her family, especially her youngest child. She has a never-ending to-do list but knows she must also make time to take care of herself. Timothy seems oblivious to it all.

Her public persona firmly in place, she smiles and all appears well in her world. However, the tension in her home is palpable. Her children feel and see and hear it. Lately, Shelly and Timothy have always been either arguing loudly or giving each other the silent treatment.

She's repeatedly suggested counseling. He's opposed to it. The week before she broke down and talked to me, she found herself researching divorce attorneys in her area. It's not what she wants. The "D" word was never a part of her dream. But what she knows for sure is that she cannot go on living like she does. She deserves better. She's tried to bring Timothy around. She tries to support him and help him be the husband she imagined he would be, but something must give, and it won't be her. She told me, "If Timothy would just love and support me like he is supposed to, we could turn this all around and build a great future together."

In over two decades of working with and coaching women, I have heard Shelly's story more times than I can share in this space. Sadly, I've been there myself. My husband would tell you that we were barely three months into our marriage when I asked for a divorce. I figured it was best to cut our losses before we brought any children into our union. I had thought it out. I was a young attorney with a bright future and he was a physician who would certainly do well for himself, so neither of us would have been overly inconvenienced by the separation. I wasn't even mad at him; I just knew that the reality of my marriage wasn't the dream I had imagined, and I was doing us both a favor by ending it early. Fast forward a couple of decades, and by the time you read this book, my husband and I will have celebrated our twentieth wedding anniversary. It hasn't all been smooth sailing, but that's life, isn't it? Birthing and raising our five children isn't always a walk on the beach, but these have been two of the most rewarding aspects of my life.

The truth is that greatness often requires greater sacrifices of us than we think possible. That thing we desire the most, if we follow through, will cause us to go to depths and heights previously unknown, but the outcome is that we become better versions of ourselves. The great poet and author Maya Angelou said, "You may encounter many defeats, but you must not be defeated. In fact, it may be necessary to encounter the defeats, so you can know who you are, what you can rise from, how you can still come out of it."

YOU ARE MAGNIFICENT.
ALWAYS HAVE BEEN AND ALWAYS WILL BE.

I am writing this book for women like me and Shelly. Women who are good-hearted and genuinely want the best for their lives, their marriages, and their children. Women who've dreamed sweet dreams but seem to be living their version of a nightmare. Women who are tired of being frustrated and are committed to finding their peace. This book will provide you with insight and the tools to examine your dreams and create the life you really desire. If you are anything like some of my clients, many of you will use these tools to rebuild your marriages. The great news is that, regardless of the outcome of your marriage, 100 percent of you will employ these instruments to create a much healthier, happier, and more peaceful you.

I am simply giddy with anticipation for the growth we will each experience on this journey. This book will take you on an expedition into yourself. It will give you an opportunity to reimagine and to invigorate your true dreams for every aspect of your life; it will literally transform your entire being. We will take off the limits, discard the voices of doom and of the naysayers, face our fears, embrace the layers we've built up over time, and see ourselves and our experiences for what they really are.

You will laugh, you will cry, and you may even have moments of anger or times when you just want to quit and throw this book in the trash, but you will stay on the journey. You will gather your faith, discover and hone your innate talents, and reclaim your personal power - the power to lead yourself to unapologetically be who you are and to create and live your own joy in any circumstance.

Though it may be scary, I hope you can get excited about giving up your indecision, blame, pain, regret, and fear to step into your magnificent future. And magnificent it is indeed because, despite your current circumstances, you are magnificent, always have been and always will be.

What I know beyond a doubt is that you are a high-achieving woman who is ready for change. You want to trust me—or you wouldn't be reading this book—but you have some concerns. What will this journey require of you? Will the outcome be worth it? As you read this book, I will ask you to reflect, journal, complete some exercises, and try some new ways of thinking about and responding to your challenges. I will encourage you to defy any thought patterns that have not served and do not serve your dreams, and I will be here to support you every step of the way.

Now, let's reclaim your life and manifest your dreams.

CHAPTER ONE:
I WANT A DIVORCE

*All relationships are important because they reveal the true
nature of the relationship we have with ourselves.*

—Robert Tew

I must admit, I have watched my fair share of movies. I enjoy a good
drama; I've even written a play or two myself. I am also an attorney,
trained to run scenarios through my mind to be able to anticipate
and plan for all possible responses from those whom I am interro-
gating. So, in true attorney fashion, after thinking through my very
young marriage and concluding that divorce was our best option, I
played out in my mind the scene of how I would break this to my
husband:

ME: Sweetheart, we need to talk.

HIM: Uhmmm.... sure. Is everything okay?

ME: (*Calm with no hint of the gravity of what I was about to
share.*) Let's take a walk.

HIM: (*Puzzled.*) Okay.

ME: You know you are a great guy. These past couple of months with you have been beautiful. I've learned so much about myself and I just want you to know how much I appreciate you.

HIM: I appreciate you, too. I had given up hope of finding someone like you.

ME: (*Interrupting him because I need to curtail the mushiness and let him down gently.*) Our marriage has really helped me to better understand myself, and what I can clearly see now is that I am not marriage material. I am not designed to be a wife. This is not about you. It is about me. You are a great guy.

HIM: So, what are you saying? What do you mean by you are not marriage material? (*He's stopped walking and is staring me intently in the eye.*)

ME: As I said, I am not designed to be a wife. I don't want to have to tell you what I am doing and where I am going or run my plans by you. I want a divorce. We have no children. We have no assets together. We can make a clean break and just be friends.

HIM: (*Vacillating between shock and hurt.*) Aya, I love you. I can't believe you are saying this. You are just going to quit on our marriage, just like that?

ME: (*Tears streaming down my face.*) I never meant to hurt you. It's me. Not you. You are an amazing man and I am so grateful you picked me, but I am just not cut out to be a wife. This is for the best. I love you.

The scene was supposed to end with us hugging and crying and then going out to dinner and talking over the good times. He would agree to the divorce and we would carry on as friends, with me even introducing him to some great female acquaintances. I did say I can be a bit dramatic, didn't I?

Well, it didn't quite work out that way. I had planned for two responses from my husband. One was resignation. I knew what I wanted, and he would realize there was no sense in even attempting to talk me out of it. The second was anger. I was prepared for any kind of outburst, or even that type of anger that causes people to withdraw into themselves, at least temporarily. What I hadn't anticipated was his *actual* response.

We did go on the walk as I had planned. I indeed stated my case and asked for a divorce. He paused upon hearing my request and simply said, "I don't do divorce. Tell me what I need to change and I'll do it." I was flabbergasted. Then I was livid. Who the hell was he to tell me he doesn't do divorce? I want what I want and he can't make me stay in a marriage I don't want. While I lost it, he stayed calm. I felt like I had been outmaneuvered in a courtroom. I wasn't prepared for his response and I honestly did not have an answer to his question. What did I want him to change?

We didn't get a divorce. As a matter of fact, as I write this, we are a few weeks away from our twentieth wedding anniversary, and I can truthfully say that my love and respect for my husband continues to grow. I am more attracted to him now than ever before. How is this even possible? What changed? How did we turn our marriage around?

We were at a crossroads. At every crossroads, there is a decision to make. You can give up, or you can choose to fight for the life you believe is possible for you. My husband had chosen to fight for our marriage vows. I decided to fight, too, but I didn't want to stay married just for the sake of being married. If we were going to keep our marriage, I wanted a commitment to build a great one. I wanted it all—intimacy, passion, great kids, spiritual growth, and a lifestyle that allowed us to give generously of our time and resources. But how were we to get there from where we were? Wishing wasn't going to make it happen. We both had to embrace love and faith, and to commit to growing ourselves, individually and together, so we could grow our marriage.

> ## WHILE WE WERE BOTH GOOD PEOPLE COMMITTED TO OUR MARRIAGE, THAT DIDN'T MEAN WE WERE WELL-EQUIPPED FOR THE CHALLENGES OF MARRIAGE.

We initially didn't seek outside help, probably out of pride. Our pride has been both a saving grace and an Achilles' heel in our marriage. Without even consciously making the decision, in my despair, I grasped onto my faith and the values instilled in me by my parents. I had watched them fight for their marriage, and it made me strongly believe that every great thing is worth making an effort for. My husband and I had two solid things going for us—our shared faith and our similar value systems. You may be thinking, "Great for you, but you don't know my situation." That is true. However, experience has shown me that every couple, if they look hard enough, can come up with a life raft or buoy to keep them afloat while they build a more solid foundation to their relationship, even if that foundation is just a friendship and not a marriage.

My husband and I recommitted to seeking God. We both agreed to completely take divorce off the table as an option in our marriage. We prayed together and committed to being kinder to and more considerate of each other. That worked for a while, but then life came at us fast and hard; we found ourselves knocked back into raging waves and our feet could not find land.

While we were both good people committed to our marriage, that didn't mean we were well-equipped for its challenges. We had sought out virtually zero premarital counseling, we weren't being mentored by a more established couple, and we didn't share our "dirty laundry" with any of the couples with whom we interacted. Our ignorance of the need for basic skillsets helpful in marriage—like effective communication, conflict resolution, money management, and how to grow intimacy—presented significant hurdles we didn't even recognize we had. We just played out what we had observed around us.

I remember one day when I ended up sitting in our guest room crying my eyes out. I felt lonely, misunderstood, overwhelmed, and beaten down. My husband was frustrated. He had repeatedly shared that he didn't think anything he did was good enough for me. His original question hung between us—what do you want me to change? I resented him for putting the onus on me to tell him what it would take to make our marriage right. Why did all the heavy lifting always end up on me? Why couldn't he figure it out and just do it? I was working sixty-plus-hour weeks building my career. By that time, I was the primary caregiver for our toddler. To compound matters, we had just suffered our second miscarriage. When did I get a break? I was in full victim mode and he was the villain. He was the callous, uncaring man who shared my bed, but not my burdens. That was my mindset . . . not a very positive one. I can assure you that it is infinitely tougher to turn things around when your mindset is negative. You cannot plant beans and harvest corn. You cannot stay in a negative mindset and expect positive outcomes in your life.

Looking back at that time in our lives, I can see now that we were both in over our heads. I came into my marriage with quite a bit of emotional baggage. Amongst other things, I was a survivor of childhood sexual abuse. I had also accumulated my fair share of betrayal by men I had trusted, prompting me to put up walls which blindsided my husband repeatedly. He, too, came into the marriage carrying his own burdens. Without a common understanding of our issues, we poked at each other's sore spots over and over again despite our best efforts. It made for a very painful time. But our pride wouldn't let us give up on ourselves or our marriage. Outwardly, we looked good. Inwardly, we kept fighting for what we knew was possible, even if we didn't have a roadmap to get there.

Life threw some more curveballs our way. We suffered four consecutive miscarriages. As strange as it may sound, our grief stripped us of everything. Our fancy education and titles couldn't save our babies. Nothing external really mattered. Broken as he was, my husband did everything he could to comfort and support me. I was at yet another crossroads. In my grief at all the loss I had endured, I contemplated suicide. But the love and concern from my husband and my love for our only living child wouldn't let me take that fatal step. I again decided to fight for my dream. In my dream, my life mattered. In my dream, I lived what I preached and I led by example. In my dream, I was at peace with myself. In my dream, I had a thriving marriage that encouraged others to build thriving marriages too.

We began to attend marriage conferences while I read many books on marriage and communication. I learned that, while I had spent the first four years of our marriage focused on what I perceived to be my husband's shortcomings, to achieve the marriage of my dreams I had to shift my focus to myself. I had to better understand myself and put in the work to heal from my past hurts. The reason I could never come up with a satisfactory answer to the question my husband had posed all those years ago was because I didn't even really know what I needed myself, and my needs changed by the moment. I was asking him to do the "heart" work which only I could do for myself. As much as he loved me, he couldn't heal me. That task was up to me and the extent to which I submitted to God.

You would think that once I had this understanding all would be well with us 100 percent of the time. Well, that was not the case at all. Certainly we had longer spells of marital bliss, but bad habits die hard, especially when there is no conscious decision to replace those with healthier ones. In other words, it is not enough to identify what you need to start doing (or do more of) in your marriage; you also have to identify what you must stop doing. Intellectually, I understood the changes I needed to make in my marriage and I very actively pursued my personal development; however, there was still the part of me which rationalized that I was doing the lion's share of the work, and I resented my husband for not being as committed to his personal development as I felt he should be.

Over the years, I have applied lessons gleaned from conferences, retreats, books, and more successful couples. I realized I was afraid of being vulnerable, of putting so much effort into something for which there are no guarantees. It was unfamiliar territory for me. I know how to study and rack up degrees. I earned four in just seven years from The Ohio State University, including a Master's degree and a Juris Doctorate. I know how to show up and deliver at work. I know how to discipline myself and get into great shape, even after five live births and four miscarriages. Those outcomes I could control, but I couldn't guarantee my dream for my marriage. It wasn't just up to me. I had to admit I was afraid of failing.

But you already know that knowing a thing and doing it consistently are completely different matters. In the next few chapters, I will share the specific strategies that have served me and my marriage the best. All these, collectively, have made a huge difference, but there is one in particular that was a complete game changer for me. I never even told my husband what I was doing, but the transformation in myself and in our marriage has been nothing short of a miracle.

> **HAVING A SUCCESSFUL MARRIAGE IS VERY MUCH LIKE RIDING A BICYCLE. YOU ALWAYS HAVE TO MAKE ADJUSTMENTS.**

This was my game changer: I learned that having a successful marriage is very much like riding a bicycle. No matter how long you've been at it, you know you always have to work on keeping your balance. There are those slight checks you constantly make to ensure you don't hit the pavement hard. You may temporarily take your hands off the bars and your feet off the pedals, but sooner rather than later you will need to get them back in place to avert a crash. It never changes. More experienced riders can coast a little longer, but they still have to make the necessary adjustments. As the Tour de France teaches us year after year, under tough conditions even the most experienced of riders can take a fall with grave consequences. Your marriage may not have been hit by the loss of children like ours was. Maybe your challenge is in the form of infidelity, financial hardships, health concerns, deployments, wayward children, addictions, poor communication, and so forth. Whatever your trials, though, believe that there is value in adversity, and meaning in facing a trial and overcoming it.

You are most likely reading this book because your marriage is already in trouble. Don't despair. Don't give up. I wrote this book just for you. This is the book I wish I had read all those years when I thought I was all alone and no one understood my situation. I have written a book designed to uplift and give you clarity on what you really want and how to achieve it.

NOTES

CHAPTER TWO:
IS YOUR MARRIAGE DESTINED
FOR FAILURE?

People do not get married planning to divorce. Divorce is the result of
a lack of preparation for marriage and the failure to learn the skills of
working together as teammates in an intimate relationship.

—Gary Chapman,
Things I Wish I'd Known Before We Got Married

If there's anything I want you to get from this chapter, it is that winners—and that's who I know you are—don't live their lives aiming for or expecting failure. Winners face the same challenges and obstacles others do, but at some point, they make up their minds to be overcomers and not just victims of their circumstances. The hurdles you are facing—or, in the case of those of you who are reading this book proactively, the ones you will face—are nothing new. What really matters is how you want to show up in your life and in your marriage.

I encourage you to read through this chapter once in its entirety and then go back and read through it again; the second time, pause to journal your responses to the questions posed and the information presented. Personalizing this experience will enable you to gain insights for your specific circumstances which you might otherwise miss.

One of my favorite Bible verses, Ecclesiastes 1:9, states, "What has been will be again, what has been done will be done again; there is nothing new under the sun." I draw a lot of hope from that verse: I understand that what I am facing, no matter how debilitating, has been faced and conquered by others. I may allow myself a small pity party, but then my attention must shift to figuring out what the overcomers did to achieve their desired outcome. I then need to decide what my desired outcome is and what I have control over, and take appropriate action.

A cursory look at marriage statistics indicates that, for areas where marriage and divorce rates have been tracked, 40–50 percent of all first marriages end in divorce. The numbers actually increase for subsequent marriages. When we factor in the 35–40 percent of married couples indicating they are not happy in their marriages, one can begin to wonder at the odds of staying married and living happily ever after.

> **WHO IS LIVING THE LIFE YOU IMAGINED FOR YOURSELF? WAS IT JUST THE LUCK OF THE DRAW OR ARE THERE THINGS THEY MAY BE DOING DIFFERENTLY?**

Who is living the life you imagined for yourself? When you look at them, was it just the luck of the draw or are there things they may be doing differently? You want that great marriage with a man who takes care of himself and is your equal partner in the marriage. You want a man who adores you and is unafraid to pursue his dreams while still giving you the support to pursue yours as you build your family together. Do you really believe this dream is possible? Do you believe it is possible for you? What's the alternative? What happens if you continue down the path you are on right now?

Amber is a client I worked with a few years ago. We met at a conference and I was immediately impressed with her poise and drive. After she found out what I do for a living, she decided to hire me as her coach to help her "gracefully transition" out of her marriage. Our conversation that evening went as follows:

ME: So, you want to transition out of your marriage?

AMBER: Yes, I am done. I can't deal with the drama anymore. We fight constantly. He married the wrong woman. He needs to treat me as an equal.

ME: Did you marry the wrong man?

AMBER: I didn't think so. We had a lot going for us, but then I should have known better.

ME: Known what better?

AMBER: I can't think of one marriage I saw growing up that I would want to emulate. How many marriages end in divorce? And of the ones who stay married, most are miserable. Marriage is no joke, and I guess I am just not cut out to do what these women do to stay married.

ME: I can relate. I've felt that way in the past. What exactly is it that married women do that you are unwilling to do?

AMBER: Choke on my words to keep the peace. Bury my dreams. Sacrifice my career. Be treated like a servant for the rest of my life. Be unappreciated. Work hard to contribute but get no respect. Raise my husband as well as our kids. Massage his ego all the time. I don't want the stress. Women are dying from the stress of being married.

ME: Wow! When you put it like that, I can see why you want out. Is there another way to look at this whole situation?

AMBER: What other way? Are you happily married?

ME: Today, I am. There have been times when my answer would have been no. I am working to ensure that tomorrow I can still claim to be happy and fulfilled in my marriage, as well as in other aspects of my life. Hey, how was college for you?

AMBER: College? Challenging, but I did okay. Why?

ME: Have you heard the statistics on the graduation and dropout rates for college students?

AMBER: Yes. It's amazing that so many kids drop out.

ME: Why didn't you drop out of college when it got challenging?

AMBER: That would have been silly. I had a goal, and I never expected college to be a cakewalk. Those challenges made me dig deeper. I now know I can hold my own and overcome anything.

ME: Anything?

AMBER: Uggggghh! Are you trying to talk me out of a divorce? It won't work. I've made up my mind.

ME: (*Silence.*)

AMBER: You don't know what I've been through. The last few years have been hell. It is taking a toll on my health, my job, and even my children! I've bent over backward to make this marriage work, and what do I have to show for it?

ME: (*Silence.*)

AMBER: I can't keep on living this way.

ME: I agree.

AMBER: You agree? So, what should I do now?

ME: What should you do now, Amber?

AMBER: I need time to reevaluate. I need to look at this differently to see how I can change things. I am just so mad at him right now.

ME: What did you do when things got challenging in college?

AMBER: I got help.

ME: Help with what?

AMBER: (*Looking at me like I asked a stupid question.*) Help in the areas where I was struggling.

ME: What happened to the students who didn't get help?

AMBER: (*Sighing.*) They flunked out. But this is different. Marriage takes two. I can get all the help I want, but if he isn't on the same page it won't work. He has to meet me halfway.

ME: What if this isn't about him? A wise woman once said, "I need to look at this differently to see how I can change things." Are you ready to follow that advice?

AMBER: What wise woman?

ME: You.

Amber's situation is not at all unusual. Most little girls grow up with the dream of being married and living happily ever after. For the most part, society expects us to get married. Certainly the literature we read as little girls reinforces that our happiness, especially as girls, is directly tied to our romantic relationships. Growing up, I would hear the phrase, "A woman is incomplete without a man." What phrases did you hear that may have impacted how you view yourself and the institution of marriage?

In many parts of the world, the inferiority of females is still promulgated, and the so-called developed nations are no exception to this historical truth. The weight of this expectation is exacerbated by the experiences of unhappy and oppressed wives. These realities beg the questions: Does happily ever after really exist beyond fairy tales?

Should we dare to hope for more for our marriages? Who determines what happily ever after looks like? Can a woman choosing to play the traditional female role in a marriage be truly happy? Can a man treat his wife as an equal and still be esteemed? What are the rules for marriages today? Should we take the "I can do better by myself" route, acquiesce and just play dead to appease society and maintain peace, or fight what many believe is a losing battle? Are there any other alternatives? If so, what are they for you?

Social Framework for Marriage Success

Why do marriages fail or succeed? Why are some able to build happy marriages while others aren't? What can we learn from happy marriages and what lessons do the "failed" marriages teach us? Thankfully, we don't have to guess at the answers. Just as research gives us clues as to what may predispose us to certain illnesses, it also provides us with some time-proven truths worth examining as we continue this journey to creating the marriage and life of your dreams. We will look at factors influencing marriage outcomes prior to and during the marriage, many of which were touched on by Amber.

Shared Values

This is part of the glue that held and continues to hold my marriage together. My husband and I both come from backgrounds in which marriage is valued. His parents remained married until my father-in-law's death. My parents recently celebrated their fifty-second wedding anniversary. We also share a common faith. As Christians, both of us believe in the sanctity of marriage—even though I had initially asked for a divorce—and in the power of God to turn any situation around. If we were totally depending on *our* willpower to resolve our marital differences, we would be divorced right now.

While we often hear that opposites attract, when it comes to values, the more closely aligned a husband and wife are, the more likely they are to build a strong marriage. The shared values serve not just as glue, but also as a foundational reference for a couple's choices and decisions. What values do you and your spouse or spouse-to-be share?

Parents' Marriage

Research shows that couples whose parents were happily married are more likely to build happy marriages, too. Much like how children of pro athletes have a jump start on excelling at their parent's sport over their equally talented peers, children learn from observing their parents and inadvertently pick up and practice tools that aid in building strong and happy relationships. Whereas these tools seem innate to them because they were modeled in their home, others may have to be proactive about learning and applying these tools.

Childhood

The more "normal" and happier their childhood, the better a child's chances at creating a happy marriage. This one should be a no-brainer. Trauma distorts how people see and interact with the world. If a person had a tough childhood, they may end up being more self-contained, less trusting, and more defensive—none of which are particularly helpful in building a happy marriage. Our experiences during our formative years form the lenses through which we perceive and relate with the world.

Age and Length of Acquaintance

The younger a couple is when they get married, particularly if they are under twenty years of age, the more likely their marriage is to end in divorce. If mature adults have a hard time dealing with the stressors of life and marriage, how much harder of a time will kids have? Scientists say that the average brain doesn't fully mature until age twenty-six or thereabouts. In other words, the younger the couple, the higher the probability of immaturity, which will compound any marital challenges. Research also shows that couples who had known each other for over a year prior to marriage have more successful marriages than others, as they are more likely to have encountered and addressed issues of compatibility which might otherwise cause a marriage to fail.

Reasons for Marriage

The reasons a couple gets married can impact the quality of their marriage. I have clients who got married just to get out of their parents' home. I know a few who chose marriage because they got more benefits from the Army as a married soldier. Some people do it for the money, others because they were pregnant and it was the proper thing to do. However, 50 percent of marriages based on premarital pregnancies end in divorce within five years, while marriages based on other such reasons, like the ones listed above, have a similarly grim outlook. Marriages built on genuine love, with a couple who care for each another and rationally decide to get married after due consideration, tend to fare better in the long run.

Parental Approval

The myth of the evil mother-in-law may be entrenched in folklore, but it is true that when the parents of your spouse disapprove of you, it does put an additional strain on the marriage. All marriages need support, and when support is not forthcoming, or worse, if your in-laws are actively opposed to you, the impact can be significant. It is worth noting that sometimes, parents disapprove of a marriage because they see traits or warning signs which the couple may be ignoring.

Stages of Marriage

Once a couple is married, there are yet other stressors that may influence the well-being and outcome of their union. I believe it is instructive to examine marriage as detailed in the book *The 7 Stages of Marriage: Laughter, Intimacy, and Passion Today, Tomorrow, Forever* by Rita DeMaria and Sari Harrar. When couples have a more realistic perspective on the challenges they may face in their marriage, they can be better prepared to safeguard their union.

> ### Many couples spend more time planning their weddings versus their marriage.

One of the most popular books for pregnant women is *What to Expect When You Are Expecting*. Even though many expectant mothers have witnessed others go through pregnancies, I still see them poring over that book, as did I. As a result of this preparation, most women are not caught unaware by things like morning sickness (or even all-day sickness). They may not like it, but they know that, if they persevere, this too shall eventually pass. Although I have heard women complain about heartburn during pregnancy, I have never met one who decided her baby wasn't worth birthing because she was tired of the heartburn. Instead, they make adjustments in themselves. How can we apply this same perspective to marriage? I have observed many couples spending more time planning their weddings than they do talking through their expectations of marriage. What do we really know about marriage and the challenges inherent in it? Why are we suffering unnecessary angst over the dissonance between our expectations and the reality of bringing two people together to function as one for the rest of their lives?

The seven stages of marriage, according to Harrar and DeMaria, are: Passion, Realization, Rebellion, Cooperation, Reunion, Explosion, and Completion. While not all couples will experience all these stages in their marriage, and certainly not necessarily in this order, a better understanding of these stages provides insights which may enable a couple to avert possible conflicts.

Passion

At this stage, the couple sees each other with rose-colored glasses. Everything feels, smells, looks, and tastes great. They are in love and the other can do no wrong.

Realization

In this stage, one or both spouses are beginning to realize and focus on the imperfections and shortcomings of the other. You may find yourself irritated by how he chews his food. He may be annoyed about your morning routine. Little things suddenly become a big deal. Can you recall a time when you or your spouse began to nitpick on each other's habits?

Rebellion

Also known as the power struggle stage. One or both spouses start to rebel in response to the criticism they feel they are unfairly subjected to by their spouse. Communication breaks down and arguments intensify during this stage.

Cooperation

If a couple stays in the rebellion stage long enough, it not only lends itself to an unhappy marriage but can also result in divorce. Some marriages are saved by the cooperation stage where the couple takes the focus off each other and place it on their kids, their careers, their business dreams, their finances, and so on. In this stage, they operate more as business partners, or even siblings, than they do as husband and wife. But it is a tenuous place to remain in. It can lead to extra-marital affairs because when emotional and sexual needs are not met within a marriage, some will seek to satisfy those needs outside of the marriage.

Reunion

The reunion stage is most common amongst empty nesters and other couples who are experiencing relief from some outward pressure. This newfound freedom gives them more time to spend with and focus on each other and to rekindle their passion.

Explosion

Unfortunately, life can be quite unpredictable. In this stage, couples typically suffer a major setback. It could be in the form of illness, poor choices by an adult child with legal ramifications, a loss of income, the death of a parent, etc. This is a time when couples can either draw closer to each other or pull apart as they individually deal with the setback.

Completion

The completion stage is the sweet spot of all marriages. Here, couples enjoy security and stability. They are completely committed to with the right mindset to enjoy each other and the life they've created.

Internal and External Marriage Stressors

Once a couple has made the decision to get married, there are still yet other stressors on their marriage. How they handle this stress makes all the difference in what kind of marriage they have and if they stay together.

> ## EVEN LOVING MARRIAGES CAN BE DERAILED BY UNEXPECTED PRESSURE. WHAT YOU DON'T KNOW CAN HURT YOUR MARRIAGE.

Familiarity

Growing up, I would often hear the phrase "Familiarity breeds contempt." Although the goal in marriage is to become so comfortable with one another that you can just be yourself and be accepted for who you are, just as you are, sometimes that level of comfort translates to people who stop concerning themselves with how they are coming across to their spouse. I once heard an otherwise-successful man describe himself as "the poster child for husbands of wives who just don't give a damn anymore." The audience laughed as I winced at the pain behind those words, for both him and her.

Parenthood

Children are certainly a blessing, but they also exert a tremendous amount of stress on marriages. It's challenging enough to juggle marriage and building a career. When you add a child to the equation, it puts an additional strain on time and finances and will quickly expose any differences in parenting styles. As sweet as children are, they are also very astute manipulators and will be sure to capitalize on any rifts in the seam of your marriage.

Finances

Most experts list money as the number one cause for divorce. Our attitudes about and skills in making and managing money can cause serious stress on a marriage.

Attitudes and Personality Types

That "A" word always seems to make an appearance, and deservedly so. A bad attitude will derail *any* marriage. An attitude of superiority and a lack of a spirit of compromise will cause your spouse to rebel or to shrink. Either way, the outcome is resentment, and resentment is a harbinger of greater marital problems. Differences in personalities affect how people communicate, and when communication breaks down, a relationship is typically doomed.

Marital Roles

We each come into marriage with preconceived notions of what role each spouse will play. What stresses a marriage isn't necessarily whether the roles are based on tradition or are more contemporary. The negative stress occurs when there is conflict over who does what. I have seen marriages where the wife is perfectly happy and fulfilled in being the caregiver, the only one who cooks and takes care of the housework, while her husband's responsibility is the lawn, the repairs, the cars, finances, etc. There are also happy marriages where all the roles are shared equally. The problem arises when one spouse has an unmet expectation or feels there is a lack of consideration on the part of the other spouse.

Sexual Expectations

Need I say more? Many couples find themselves dealing with mismatched libidos and differing expectations for their sex life. Add stressors like pornography and/or sexual addiction, demanding careers, financial woes, children, or illness to the mix and a couple's sex life can become nonexistent.

Major Illness or Catastrophe

There's nothing quite like a major illness or catastrophe to exert stress on a marriage. If the marriage was already frayed, this could easily be the breaking point. I have witnessed marriages ripped apart by cancer, miscarriages, or the death of a child.

Divergent Interests

As an attorney, I can assure you that it's pretty standard to include the words "irreconcilable differences" in a petition for divorce. What this is really saying is that people either never had much in common or were so focused on other interests that they grew apart. Couples with divergent interests have a harder time developing understanding and empathy for one another. This also applies to the differences that may exist in the couples' upbringing and background. The more similar their vision for their future, education, social status, ethnicity, and religion, the stronger their foundation for marriage.

Communication and Conflict Resolution

Most of us go into marriage without ever discussing how we intend to handle conflicts when they show up—and show up they will. When couples have poor communication skills, they are bound to experience more conflict and more disunity. Many of us just copy what we saw our parents do, for better or for worse. Some of us do the exact opposite of what was modeled for us, and that isn't always the best choice either.

A Strong Sense of Self

The better you know and like yourself, the easier it will be for you to stay grounded and not lose yourself in your marriage. I see many a couple who begin their married life not really ever knowing who they are, and without that strong foundation of self-knowledge and love, they are more susceptible to the stressors of marriage.

Assessing the State of Your Marriage

Moving forward, it is important to get a clearer picture of the real state of your marriage. Beyond general feelings of frustration and dissatisfaction, can you pinpoint what is and isn't working for you in your marriage? Assessing your marriage will give you the necessary information to confidently decide whether you will choose to stay on and work on your marriage or decide it is time to "cut your losses" and move on.

When you go for a medical checkup, before you even get to see the medical practitioner, you are required to fill out a series of forms designed to gather your medical history and to determine your current symptoms and reasons for seeking medical services. I must admit I am sometimes put off by the forms and the level of detail they cover. However, although answering all the questions and providing the information required is time-consuming, I understand that the more the medical practitioner understands my background and current ailments, the more accurate their diagnosis and treatment plan will be.

The same concept applies to assessing your marriage. The clearer you are on your history and the current state of your marriage, the better your ability to figure out the best way forward for you. To facilitate this process, I have compiled a survey to assist you in ascertaining your current level of marital satisfaction, as well as your perception of your spouse's level of satisfaction. The survey covers a variety of areas including intimacy, sexual satisfaction, household responsibilities, communication, quantity and quality of interaction, trust, spiritual connection, and finances. Access and download the survey at www.wivesatthecrossroads.com

You can also invite your spouse to take the survey independently and then compare your responses. The survey includes a scoring key and some recommendations based on your responses. This could be an invaluable tool for you as you decide your next steps.

Whatever your score may be on your current level of satisfaction in your marriage, remember the first point I made in this chapter: winners are not overly perturbed by statistics or the failures of others. They take stock, they learn, and they commit to success on their terms. There is indeed nothing new under the sun and no situation that can withstand the force of your being.Notes

NOTES

CHAPTER THREE:
ROADMAP TO YOUR DREAM
MARRIAGE—OVERVIEW

*All you need is the plan, the road map, and the courage
to press on to your destination.*

—Earl Nightingale

Wait! Before we dive in, it's important to me not to waste your time or mine. I am assuming you have already asked and answered the following questions for yourself, but just to be sure, I will pose them here: Why marriage? Why do you want to be married? I have asked these questions of numerous clients over the years, and the initial response I get is usually a quizzical look.

If you are like me, your parents never specifically sat you down to explain why you should get married or the benefits of marriage for you, or even what you should look for in a spouse. For me, there was an unspoken expectation that I would get married and have children, and that I would desire to do so. I was encouraged to learn how to clean and cook and excel academically so I could live a good life with my husband and children. In the society in which I was raised, I often heard things like "a woman is incomplete without a man" and "an unmarried woman can never be a happy woman." As a Christian, I was taught to "Go forth and multiply." I was twenty-six years old when I got married, and that gave me some time to expand my horizons and figure out that I did have options. I absolutely could choose whether I wanted to be married or not. My parents were actually surprised when I announced I had met someone I was considering for marriage. They'd given up hope on me. I was too opinionated and headstrong to make a good wife.

I used to fantasize about my ideal marital situation. Picture this: I would marry the man of my dreams. We would make beautiful babies. We would live in a home that had two sections connected by a hallway. I would live in one section on my own. This would be my sanctuary where I write books that will change the world. My family would not be permitted to come to my section . . . ever. I would, when it pleased me, go over to the other section where my husband and our kids reside. He would be their primary caregiver, and when I was with them I would be fully present. I did not share this fantasy with my husband before our wedding, even though I could visualize every detail of this living environment and had for years. Are you laughing yet? Is there any wonder I was ready for divorce within the first few months of my marriage?

> **I USED TO FANTASIZE ABOUT MY IDEAL MARITAL SITUATION. INTERESTINGLY, I DIDN'T SHARE THOSE FANTASIES WITH MY HUSBAND PRIOR TO OUR MARRIAGE.**

How about you? Why did you get married? What were your thoughts about marriage before you made the commitment? Did you really commit to your vows or just recite what was required of you? What did you hope to get out of your marriage? What did you hope to give? How do you feel about marriage in general? What do you consider the benefits and the drawbacks of marriage for you, for your spouse? Beyond the pain, the loneliness, the hurt, the disappointments, the anger, and the fear, is your marriage worth it? Do you really believe this?

Just in case you were wondering, here's a summary of what advocates for marriage say about the institution:

Marriage lays the foundation for families, and families are the building blocks of all society. Marriage is a life-long commitment that encourages us to grow in selflessness and love. Marriage is designed to mirror God's love for the world. Marriage serves as a safe place for sex and intimacy and is a deterrent to sexual immorality. Marriage is a defense against illness. Psychologist and author John Gottman states the benefits of being married are "better physical health, more resistance to infection, fewer infections, and a reduced likelihood of dying from cancer, from heart disease, from all major killers. The other health benefit is longevity: People live longer if they are in marital relationships, particularly if they are in good, satisfying relationships."

> ## MARRIAGE IS THE BUILDING BLOCK OF SOCIETY.

Marriage provides the ideal environment for childbearing and -rearing. Statistics abound on the effects of a father's absence in a child's life—everything from an increase in delinquency to substance abuse issues, higher probability of sexual abuse, higher incidence of mental illnesses, and higher rates of incarceration. Children raised by their own, married mother and father are less likely to be poor or to experience persistent economic insecurity, are more likely to stay in school, are likely to have fewer behavioral and attendance problems, and are more likely to earn four-year college degrees. They are also more likely to have positive attitudes toward marriage and greater success in forming lasting marriages.

A happy marriage also positively affects long-term health. Married people are healthier, happier, and enjoy longer lives than those who are not married. Not surprisingly, married mothers have lower rates of depression than single or cohabiting mothers. Marriage also impacts wealth. Married couples build more wealth on average than singles or cohabiting couples, and married women are economically better off than divorced, cohabiting, or never-married women. Also, married women are at lower risk for domestic violence than women in cohabiting or dating relationships.

Marriage even positively affects crime rates. Boys raised in single-parent homes are more likely to engage in criminal and delinquent behavior than those raised by two married, biological parents. Married women are significantly less likely to be the victims of violent crime than single or divorced women, and married men are less likely to perpetrate violent crimes than unmarried men.

I decided that I wanted all these benefits and more from my union with my husband. But I also made another decision based on my faith: unless my marriage was causing me or my children harm, I would honor the covenant I made with God the moment I said *I do*. I had no guarantees about the outcome of my efforts to improve my marriage. However, I was certain my personal growth would yield great dividends. As it stands, not only have I grown tremendously, I am now living my dream marriage—and it gets better with each passing day.

It is no coincidence that you are reading this book right now. Of all the hundreds of thousands of books on marriage and relationships, this is the one you've chosen at this point in your life. There is a reason for that choice: you are not quite ready to throw in the towel on your marriage. For as much pain and frustration as you have experienced, there is something inside of you still yearning and believing you can have your dream come true. You can be happily married to a man who loves, adores, and supports you, a man confident in himself with whom you can build a lasting legacy. I am convinced that what you believe, and have the courage to single-mindedly pursue, you will achieve. I know this to be true in my life and in the lives of my clients. What do you believe?

By the end of this chapter, I will have outlined a roadmap to your Dream Marriage. You may be expecting a how-to manual for changing your spouse, but that is not the focus of this roadmap. The real focus is you.

Shortly after our first miscarriage, my life was in turmoil. I had a toddler, a demanding career, and a husband in medical residency, which meant he practically lived at the hospital, coming home just to crash and change his clothes before his next shift. I was tired, overwhelmed, and sure that all my problems would be solved if I could just change my husband. I was smart enough to realize I didn't have the power to change him myself. The thinking that we can ever change another person gets us in trouble every time. However, I believed there was a greater power I could tap into to change him. I bought Stormie Omartian's bestseller *The Power of a Praying Wife* and eagerly dug in to find the exact formula for prayers that would transform my husband into what I felt he should be.

I didn't make it past chapter one before I threw down the book in disgust. Why? She ended the very first prayer in the book with a line I can still recall verbatim seventeen years later. She wrote, "Give my husband a new wife, and let it be me." What? I bought that book to fix *him*. I was looking for prayers that would change him. He doesn't need a new wife; he's the problem, and I certainly shouldn't be the one to have to change!

A few months later, a friend called and confided she was having marital problems. She was a fellow Christian so I recommended Stormie's book to her as a resource. Her next question caught me off guard. She asked, "Do you use the book in your marriage?" I pride myself on honesty so I chose to tell her the truth: I had not picked up the book again after the initial prayer because I was so offended that anyone could in any way imagine I wasn't already the perfect wife to my husband. Absurd, right? But that was my mindset at the time, and as I shared this with my friend, I saw myself with new eyes. My ego was raging out of control. No, my husband wasn't perfect, but then again, neither was I. I not only picked up the book again and worked through it, I have since then gone through the study guide four or five times, and the book is one I revisit annually.

You may feel the same way about some of the steps I am about to walk you through as I initially did about *The Power of a Praying Wife*. Of the six steps, only two are focused on your marriage; and even then, you and what you truly desire for yourself, regardless of your marital status, remain at the forefront of the work I will be encouraging you to do. In other words, this book is not a roadmap to changing your spouse; it's a roadmap to a better version of yourself. This is exciting and liberating.

> ## THIS BOOK IS A ROADMAP TO A BETTER VERSION OF YOU.

It means that when you work through these steps, you unshackle yourself from the chains that may have had you bound. You become a thermostat instead of a thermometer in your marriage and in your life. In other words, you choose your emotions and the meaning you attach to things, and you are no longer at the mercy of everything going on in your life. These steps are liberating if you choose to embrace them. The following is a conversation I had with a client who was uncertain about following the six steps:

TERESA: I know you mean well, but I am not sure this coaching program is what I need.

ME: Please elaborate.

TERESA: I've been working on this marriage for a long time. If there's anything I could change in me to make it better, I would have already done it.

ME: I know you believe that.

TERESA: So, you agree with me?

ME: Have you ever tried to plug in an address into your GPS only to get a message that the address cannot be located?

TERESA: Yes.

ME: That can be frustrating when you are getting confirmation from others that you have the right address. If your GPS is working, why can't it find the address you need?

TERESA: Sometimes, if the address is in a newer location, the information may not be updated for the GPS to access it.

ME: Hmmmm . . . . What has influenced your ideas about marriage and the pathways available to you to create the marriage you want?

TERESA: Well, obviously my parents and . . . Wait a minute. (*She starts laughing.*) Are you trying to say that my marriage GPS may need updating?

ME: What's your fear?

TERESA: Fear? I have no fears. No, that's not true. I am afraid. And I am upset with myself for being afraid. I am afraid of failing again. And I am tired of failing. This isn't supposed to be this hard. I keep to myself. I don't need the whole world in my business. This is all so unfair.

ME: I can relate. I've been at the crossroads. I couldn't go straight because I'd drive off a cliff. I didn't want to go back to where I had just left, and my GPS couldn't tell whether I should make a left or right turn. I needed help.

TERESA: What did you do?

ME: I called a friend who I knew had made it to the location I was looking for. She asked me just one question: Where are you now? With her guidance and support, I made it to my destination in record time.

TERESA: She had details your GPS didn't have?

ME: She'd traveled the road many times herself.

TERESA: I've seen the testimonials. I know you get results.

ME: I am a great coach and it would be an honor to coach you to your desired destination. Are you ready to trust me and the process?

TERESA: (*Sighs.*) Yes. Yes, I am.

The Roadmap to Your Dream Marriage

The roadmap to your dream marriage consists of six steps. This is a general overview; I will address each step in more detail in subsequent chapters. Don't get ahead of yourself, and please don't skip any steps.

STEP 1: WHAT DO YOU REALLY WANT?

The first step on the roadmap to creating your dream marriage is to identify clearly what you want in the first place. One of my favorite sections from *Alice in Wonderland*, a conversation between Alice and the Cheshire Cat, captures the importance of clarity of purpose:

"Would you tell me, please, which way I ought to go from here?"

"That depends a good deal on where you want to get to," said the Cat.

"I don't much care where—" said Alice.

"Then it doesn't matter which way you go," said the Cat.

"—so long as I get SOMEWHERE," Alice added as an explanation.

"Oh, you're sure to do that," said the Cat, "if you only walk long enough."

You may be used to following the beaten path or doing what is expected of you because it is the right or peaceable thing to do, but I am asking you to step up to a whole new level. If you want what you've never had before, you must be willing to do what you've never done before. Your map will be personal to you, and the path you take will be dictated by the destination you and you alone determine. If you embark on this journey without clarifying your purpose, you will meander aimlessly and compound your frustration. If you are not committed to this step, don't proceed at all.

STEP 2: WOMAN IN THE MIRROR: ASSESSING YOUR STRENGTHS AND AREAS FOR GROWTH

This step is crucial as you prepare to create and live your dream. In this step, you will take inventory of your strengths. What has worked for you in the past? Where have you had success and why? What comes easily to you? This can be a difficult step for some because it will also require you to take stock of your shortcomings, your less-desirable character traits, and the habits that have derailed you in the past. You will need to come to terms with the role you've played in creating your current life, regardless of the circumstances life has thrown at you. The great news is that, at the end of this step, you will have a clear picture of what strengths to capitalize on and of specific areas to target for growth depending on the dream you want to realize in your life.

STEP 3: LEAD YOURSELF

This is one of my favorite steps. It's empowering and exhilarating to realize you require neither ideal circumstances nor anyone else's permission to live your dream life. Amazing, isn't it? This is where

AYA FUBARA ENELI, ESQ.

you put on your Boss Lady hat and begin to take confident action in the direction of your dreams. It will encourage you to pursue your dream without the fear that you may not achieve it, because you will realize you already have access to all the tools you need to achieve your dreams. I tell you, this step is life-changing.

STEP 4: ENJOY THE INTIMACY AND SEXUAL FULFILLMENT YOU CRAVE

If step three is empowering, step four is pure ecstasy. When was the last time you felt ecstatic? When was the last time you felt sexual joy coursing through your veins? That's supposed to be one of the benefits of marriage—sexual fulfillment. In this step, you will first break through some of those barriers to true intimacy with yourself. Once you are more comfortable with yourself, it is much easier to achieve intimacy with your spouse. Get ready. Like I said, this is a fun step.

STEP 5: THE THIRTY-DAY BEST WIFE EVER PLEDGE

Step five is pure magic. I implemented this challenge in my life without alerting my husband. The transformation was nothing short of a miracle. Seriously, this step alone took our connection to a level I never even envisioned was possible. I couldn't stop thinking of my husband. It was my pleasure to anticipate and meet his needs, and the reciprocity blew my mind. Now, bad habits die hard, so there were moments when I was sorely tempted to revert to my old ways, but I persevered, and the dividends are priceless.

STEP 6: OVERCOME YOUR OBSTACLES

If you've ever started and not finished a project, if you are prone to falling prey to life's curveballs, this step is a lifesaver. The best-laid plans are often derailed by unforeseen obstacles. In this step, you will identify the most likely obstacles to creating your dream marriage, and you will create a game plan to overcome each one of them.

* * *

These Six Steps, when followed in the right order, will give you the clarity and courage to create a life that honors your dreams and the essence of who you are. No more standing frustrated at the crossroads. Embrace the roadmap to reclaim your life and create the marriage of your dreams.

NOTES

CHAPTER FOUR:
WHAT DO YOU REALLY WANT?

*Freeing yourself was one thing; claiming ownership of
that freed self was another.*

—Toni Morrison

One of my all-time favorite songs is Diana Ross' "Theme from Mahogany." The lyrics of that song challenged me as a child and still do:
Do you know where you're going to?
Do you like the things that life is showing you? Where are you going to?
Do you know?

Do you get
What you're hoping for
When you look behind you
There's no open door
What are you hoping for?
Do you know?

One of my clients, Ijeoma, did not know where to start or where she was going to: IJEOMA: Where do we start? This is all so overwhelming.

ME: I am tempted to start singing in my Maria von Trapp voice: "Let's start at the very beginning." Are you sitting?

IJEOMA: Yes.

ME: Get comfortable. Place your feet firmly on the floor and just relax. Over the course of the next few weeks, you will be taking a journey into your self—rediscovering and celebrating you and getting laser-focused on what you want and how to manifest what you desire in your life. It is going to be exhilarating and yet challenging at times, but through it all, I will be right here with you. Always remember that you are worthy of your dreams.

IJEOMA: I am worthy of my dreams.

ME: What do you want? What do you dream of?

IJEOMA: I don't know anymore. I just want peace. I am tired of all the fighting.

ME: That's understandable. The first step in creating the marriage of your dreams, or in attaining any other dream, is to get really clear on what you want and why. What do you want?

IJEOMA: Peace. Love. Support. My life. ME: Do you want your marriage? IJEOMA: I think so. Yes, I do.

ME: Why?

IJEOMA: Why? Because I've given too much and too many years. Why? Because I never thought this would be me. This isn't the life I signed up for. Why? Because I am supposed to be married!

ME: Remember the breathing exercises I taught you? Breathe. Deep breaths. IJEOMA: I want my marriage to work. I need my marriage to work.

ME: I hear you.

IJEOMA: My marriage has to work because I have no vision of my life as a single mother. I've been a wife for so long, how could I be anything else? (*Long pause.*) I can't believe I just said that.

ME: Is it the truth?

IJEOMA: The truth is that there has been so much pain for so long, I don't know what I feel or want anymore. For years, I've held on. Through the name-calling and all his selfishness, I held on. Through the loneliness and the lack of support, I held on. Through the cheating, I held on. I've trained myself to hold on and now I don't even know what I am holding on to. I don't even know what I am holding . . . . (*Voice trails off.*)

ME: When did you recognize this truth?

IJEOMA: Just now.

ME: How does this make you feel?

IJEOMA: I don't know. Sad. Confused. Angry. Afraid.

ME: I am excited for you. I am excited for you because I know the power of truth to set us free.

IJEOMA: You mean like now I can decide if I want to keep holding on? I can figure out what I am holding on to? I can see this marriage for what it is and figure out what I want it to be? I have a choice.

ME: Yes, you have a choice. I am really proud of you and your courage to do this work. How are you feeling about this journey now?

IJEOMA: Really good. I needed this more than I realized.

You may be feeling some resistance to trusting me or this process, just like Ijeoma, but I encourage you to embrace the process. As you read and work through this chapter, I am going to ask you to resist the urge to just hope things get better and I will encourage you to get really clear about what you want. What do you want? How do you envision your life? We will use a variety of tools to help you clarify what you want for your life. But first, let me explain why this first step is essential to your success.

You may have heard about the Reticular Activating System (RAS). It is a small portion of your brain that serves as the gateway through which almost all information accesses the rest of your brain. It is designed to work to achieve what you tell it is most important to you. Like breathing, it is always at work, whether you are aware of it or not. You program it by what you focus on.

It takes directions from your conscious mind (like "I need to hear my baby") and passes them on to your subconscious mind. Your subconscious mind stays on the alert to accomplish its directives. The extent to which you are intentional about the directives your conscious mind passes on to your subconscious determines, to a large degree, your ability to create the life you dream. Let's get to work determining what you really, really want for your life.

Creating a Life Purpose Statement

Your goal in reading this book is to figure out how to create your dream marriage. To do so, you must first start with an understanding of yourself. What adds meaning to your life? What is important to you? What nurtures you? Where do you want to serve and have an impact? A life purpose statement allows you to get clarity on all these questions, which helps decision-making to be more straightforward in every area of your life. Your life purpose statement will help you determine exactly what you need to do to create the marriage you desire.

What is your purpose and how are you living that out? There is a reason every successful business has a mission statement. The mission statement serves as the compass for the company. It serves as a foundation for evaluating options and determining next steps.

Just as businesses and major corporations use their mission statements to chart their way forward, every individual should also have a personal mission statement—or, as I prefer to call it, a life purpose statement.

Do you know your life purpose? Your life's purpose is the reason for your very existence. Richard Leider, author of *The Power of Purpose: Creating Meaning in Your Life and Work*, defines it as "the conscious choice of what, where, and how to make a positive contribution to our world. It is the theme, quality, or passion we choose to center our lives around." Christian life coach Tony Stoltzfus states that "life purpose is the energy of passion, channeled through experience and design in the service of a greater calling."

A life purpose statement will summarize your purpose in a single sentence that is easy to remember. This statement should include the following: your message (the what), your audience (who you will serve), your tasks (the how), and your impact (your desired end goal).

Examples of life purpose statements include:

- To empower and equip women for financial success through coaching and books.
- To help busy people eat healthier by teaching how to make quick and nutritious meals.
- To promote healing in youth through music therapy.
- To rescue children from sex trafficking through education and provision of rehabilitation services.

To create your life purpose statement, you must embark on a journey of self-discovery that few have the discipline and fortitude to complete. It is time to intimately explore who you are and to gain clarity for yourself on what matters to you. You must look within to discover your unique design. You must honestly examine your past to understand how your experiences have shaped you to live out your purpose. You must look ahead and muster the courage to develop your passions and dreams. You must look around and to your Creator to determine how to pull this all together, to create one magnificent life by reclaiming your power.

To accomplish this, you must ask and answer as many questions as possible to help you get to the core of who you are, rather than just what people have said you can be. As I was growing up, people saw my passion for justice and my ability to teach and motivate, which made most predict that I would be an attorney. I did end up earning a law degree, but over time I began to pay attention to where I am really passionate and effective. Teaching, inspiring, and coaching women and youth to live their dreams is definitely my sweet spot.

Here are sample questions you can ask to begin to better understand yourself and your life purpose. Write your answers down so you can review them and connect the dots. Take the time to write out your responses to these questions without censoring or second-guessing yourself.

Passion: What Motivates You?

- What excites you the most in life?
- What brings you joy?
- If you had only a few months to live, what would be most important for you to be and do?
- What would make your life complete?
- What makes you so mad you just want to get up and do something about it?
- What do you enjoy doing, even for no pay?
- What are the places or roles in your life that just tug at your heartstrings—that make you laugh, cry, get angry, sad, etc.?

Energy

- What are three things you've done that you couldn't wait to get at each day?
- What are three things you dread or constantly avoid?

- What always energizes you?
- What drains your energy?

Fulfillment

- When you live from your heart, what is most fulfilling to you?
- What has added the most meaning to your life? What in life gives you the greatest satisfaction?
- What accomplishments or legacies would have ultimate significance for you?
- What makes you feel fully alive when you are doing it?
- What gives you peace?

Changing the World

- What would you change in the world, if it were up to you?
- Imagine your funeral. What would you want people to say about how you lived and your impact on the world? How do you want your epitaph to read?

Design: Who Are You?

When people are asked this question, they typically respond with their job title, education, marital status, and such. For the purposes of this step, I am encouraging you to go deeper. At the core of your being, who are you? There are things we know intuitively about ourselves. I know I am deeply compassionate; it is in my DNA. What do you know about yourself?

- Where have you found real meaning in life?
- What did you dream of being when you grew up?
- What do you know intuitively that you want to be or do in life?
- What kinds of roles and responsibilities do you enjoy or are you good at?

- What roles do you avoid?
- What experiences can you employ to serve others?
- What experiences have you had that gave you a deep sense of purpose?
- What has your whole life prepared you to do?
- What do those who know you well say about what you are created to do?
- What have you done that has been most successful or most beneficial to others?
- What relationships have influenced your sense of your destiny, and how?
- Is there a common passion that was passed down to you from your parents?
- What is your family's historical legacy?
- What sense of purpose have you drawn from your culture or community?

Personality Assessments

Personality assessments are a great tool to better understand yourself, your strengths, and your weaknesses, as well as how to perform optimally. Do you know your personality type? There are many personality assessments available, including DISC, Myers-Briggs, Strengths-Finder, etc. While a full personality test is too long to include here, you can access a DISC personality test at www.Reclaimyourlifebook.com/Disc. You can also learn more about your spiritual gifts by taking an inventory found in the book (?) *Discover Your Spiritual Gifts* by C. Peter Wagner.

Life Experience

There is no such thing as a wasted life unless we choose not to learn from and apply all our life experiences. Every pain and difficulty is a qualification if you choose to make them so. For example, I am uniquely qualified to minister to women who are experiencing the pain of infertility or miscarriages, because I have suffered four miscarriages and have studied long and hard on the topic and on how to heal from such tragedies. Think about it: who can better minister to women who are feeling the sting of regret from an abortion than a woman who herself has had an abortion? Who understands better the needs of a newly released ex-offender than one who has experienced imprisonment and battled back into the social graces and acceptance of society? Think about how your experiences might shape your life purpose.

- What have your experiences prepared you to do?
- What experiences have most shaped you as an individual?
- How have your failures and shortcomings and the adversity you've experienced prepared you to serve others?
- What gifts have you gleaned from your failures?

Work Experience, Skills, and Abilities

- What knowledge or skills have you acquired in your career, paid or unpaid, that you want to incorporate as you pursue your life purpose?
- What are you most proud of accomplishing in your career?
- What are three work experiences that have readied you for your life purpose? How have they prepared you for what you were born to do?
- What are your top five skills and abilities?
- What kinds of things are people always asking you to do for them?
- What sets you apart?

Calling

A calling comes from outside of yourself, compelling you to serve something bigger than yourself. Some find their calling as they meet specific needs in society. Many find their calling as they grow in relationship with God. Others have found their calling out of painful experiences in their lives.

- What legacy do you want to leave behind?

- How will the world be a better place because you lived?

- What does a great legacy look like to you? Give an example or two of lives you truly admire.

- What are the commonalities amongst those you most frequently serve or want to serve?

- Over the last ninety days, who have you gone out of your way to help, in big or small ways? What drew you to each of these people?

* * *

Review your answers and insights and, listening to your heart, write your life purpose statement with no judgment. Don't overthink it and don't procrastinate. Draft your statement and you can then edit as you see fit. The goal is not perfection. Email us your life purpose statement and we may include it with the examples on our website. Our email address is aya@wivesatthecrossroads.com. You can also visit www.wivesatthecrossroads.com/worksheets to download a life purpose worksheet.

Congratulations! Now that you have your life purpose statement, it's time to examine all areas of your life using the Eneli Abundant Life Scale.

ENELI ABUNDANT LIFE SCALE

Date: _____

For each area, please take a moment to consider where you are and where you would like to be. In each "current state" box, briefly note the reasons you chose your number.

Emotional Health

Sense of peace and emotional stability. Level of happiness and ability to handle daily stressors.

CURRENT STATE:	DESIRED STATE:
On a scale of 1 (panic) to 10 (peak), how would you rate this area of your life? 1 2 3 4 5 6 7 8 9 10	Improvements, changes, or enhancements. What would make this area a "10" for you?

Physical Health—Nutrition, Movement, Exercise, and Rest

Include activities of daily living, like cleaning and gardening, as well as things like dancing, yoga, walking, running, and cycling, balanced with adequate rest and relaxation.

CURRENT STATE:	DESIRED STATE:
On a scale of 1 (panic) to 10 (peak), how would you rate this area of your life? 1 2 3 4 5 6 7 8 9 1 0	Improvements, changes, or enhancements. What would make this area a "10" for you?

Time and Schedule

Sense of control over one's own schedule. Ability to get important things done and still maintain balance.

CURRENT STATE:	DESIRED STATE:
On a scale of 1 (panic) to 10 (peak), how would you rate this area of your life? 1 2 3 4 5 6 7 8 9 1 0	Improvements, changes, or enhancements. What would make this area a "10" for you?

Physical Environment

Spaces where you live and work (consider light, noise, toxins, color, etc.), as well as overall surroundings of those spaces.

CURRENT STATE:	DESIRED STATE:
On a scale of 1 (panic) to 10 (peak), how would you rate this area of your life? 1 2 3 4 5 6 7 8 9 1 0	Improvements, changes, or enhancements. What would make this area a "10" for you?

Close Relationships and Communication

Spending time with loved ones, family, friends, and/or coworkers who are supportive and with whom you communicate effectively. Quality of intimate relationship with another.

CURRENT STATE:	DESIRED STATE:
On a scale of 1 (panic) to 10 (peak), how would you rate this area of your life? 1 2 3 4 5 6 7 8 9 10	Improvements, changes, or enhancements. What would make this area a "10" for you?

Spiritual Health

Seeing purpose and meaning in something larger than one's self; may include relationship with God or other religious affiliation.

CURRENT STATE:	DESIRED STATE:
On a scale of 1 (panic) to 10 (peak), how would you rate this area of your life? 1 2 3 4 5 6 7 8 9 10	Improvements, changes, or enhancements. What would make this area a "10" for you?

Personal and Professional Development

Growing and developing one's own abilities, talents, and interests, both in *being* and *doing*, and living with both in balance.

CURRENT STATE:	DESIRED STATE:
On a scale of 1 (panic) to 10 (peak), how would you rate this area of your life? 1 2 3 4 5 6 7 8 9 1 0	Improvements, changes, or enhancements. What would make this area a "10" for you?

Recreation and Fun

Devoting adequate time and resources to balancing life's demands with recreation and fun

CURRENT STATE:	DESIRED STATE:
On a scale of 1 (panic) to 10 (peak), how would you rate this area of your life? 1 2 3 4 5 6 7 8 9 1 0	Improvements, changes, or enhancements. What would make this area a "10" for you?

Financial Stability

Confidence in effectively handling finances, covering everyday expenses, and saving for future needs.

CURRENT STATE:	DESIRED STATE:
On a scale of 1 (panic) to 10 (peak), how would you rate this area of your life? 1 2 3 4 5 6 7 8 9 10	Improvements, changes, or enhancements. What would make this area a "10" for you?

Career and Profession

Satisfaction with career/profession and its progression and ability to meet your future goals.

CURRENT STATE:	DESIRED STATE:
On a scale of 1 (panic) to 10 (peak), how would you rate this area of your life? 1 2 3 4 5 6 7 8 9 10	Improvements, changes, or enhancements. What would make this area a "10" for you?

Abundant Life Scale Score (Circle Your Score):

1–30 = Crisis Living Level 31–50 = Unhealthy Living Level
51–75 = Healthy Living Level 76–100 = Optimal Living Level

If your score is a 50 or less, I encourage you to speak to a certified life coach or counselor immediately.

Adapted from Bain's Life Success Scale, found at www.DwightBain.com, and Duke University's Health Coaching Desired Outcomes Survey © 2011, www.ayaeneli.com

Setting Goals

What areas have you identified as strengths for you? What surprised you about your responses to the Eneli Abundant Life Scale? As you move forward in this section, please pay attention to how your responses can inform the goals you set for yourself.

To create your dream marriage, you must get into the habit of not just knowing what you want, but also of setting and achieving goals for your life. Experts claim that fewer than 20 percent of people ever write down their goals. It is my hope that you will make goal setting and implementation a major part of your life. In this section, you will write at least one goal for each of the eight life areas listed below.

The eight life areas you should focus on are: career/vocation, money, living environment, personal growth, health and recreation, community, family, and spirituality. It is important that you set goals for every aspect of your life. What do you want for yourself financially? What are your personal growth goals, and how will you accomplish them? What do you desire for your health? How do you envision your career? Where and how do you want to live? Clarity is power. Get clear about what *you* want for *your* life regardless of what may or may not be happening in your marriage.

> CLARITY IS POWER. GET CLEAR ABOUT WHAT YOU WANT FOR YOUR LIFE REGARDLESS OF WHAT MAY OR MAY NOT BE HAPPENING IN YOUR MARRIAGE.

Years ago, I was coaching a business executive in her early fifties. Pat had hired me to help her figure out why her earnings had plateaued even though she was working harder. She was initially resistant to creating either a purpose statement for her life or goals for any area of her life other than her business. In her words, "The rest of my life is great. I just needed a coach to help me take my business to the next level." Pat finally agreed to "humor me" and work on writing out her goals for the other areas of her life. To her surprise, once she had her goals written down, she was able to observe for herself just how out of balance her life was. She was overextended and stressed out and had been neglecting her health for years. To overcome the effects of an ugly divorce, she had created some impossible-to-achieve rules for any other serious relationships.

Over the course of a year of working together, she dropped over twenty pounds. Her physician took her off some medication she had been on since her thirties. She lightened her commitments and freed up time to be more innovative with her business, and as a result she increased her earnings that year by $90,000 over the previous years. Why would there be such remarkable results? I liken it to driving a car with three new tires and a flat tire. Not only will you not travel very far, the journey will be very bumpy and will eventually damage other parts of the car. While you may have picked up this book to focus on your marriage, real success is tied to taking a complete look at yourself and at all aspects of your life. Everything is connected. You cannot compartmentalize your life without eventually dealing with the consequences of that decision. So, as much as you may want to skip over or rush this step, you owe it to yourself to do the work and do it with excellence.

> **A GOAL IS A CRYSTALLIZED VISION OF WHO YOU WANT TO BE, WHERE YOU WANT TO GO, AND WHAT YOU WANT TO HAVE, GIVE, OR EXPERIENCE, WITH A SPECIFIC DEADLINE.**

A goal is a crystallized vision of who you want to be, where you want to go, and what you want to have, give, or experience, with a specific deadline. Goal setting builds a bridge and a clear path from today's dream to tomorrow's reality. Goal setting maximizes your chance of creating and living a successful life. Goal setting ensures that you are actually working to create the life you want, instead of what someone else wants for you. To effectively write and accomplish your goals, consider the following guidelines:

- Develop a clear and compelling vision for your life. This is where your life purpose statement gives you an advantage.

- Write down your goals with a plan, one positively stated in the present tense.

- Identify personality changes necessary for your success. Remember, to have what you've never had, you must do what you've never done.

- Get a coach. In the words of bestselling author Andy Stanley, "You will never maximize your potential in any area without coaching. It is impossible."

- Review your goal progress often and make adjustments as necessary.

If you choose to live without setting and following through on your goals, you are giving up your power to create the life you dream. It is important to recognize that you must either fully participate in your life or resign yourself to the mercy of others. When you set goals and review them consistently, you engage your Reticular Activating System to go to work on your behalf.

The History of Your Future Marriage

One of my favorite tools for engaging my brain to bring about my deepest desires is to visualize the history of my life. Successful people repeatedly talk about envisioning their success. Athlete after athlete will tell you they had seen themselves making the game-winning shot or had dreamed of hoisting the trophy long before it happened.

Actors will share how they practiced acceptance speeches when they were still unknown and unappreciated.

Think about it this way: have you ever had a dream so real that your heart was racing, you woke up drenched in sweat, and you were absolutely convinced you just lived through the experience when in actuality it was just a dream? Your brain thought it was real and so your body responded accordingly. Have you ever watched a movie and, although you knew it wasn't real, found yourself crying and feeling every emotion of the character on the screen? Now, imagine using that to your benefit. You can visualize your desired outcome and make it happen.

So let us take a journey together. Go somewhere quiet and eliminate as many distractions as possible. Get into a comfortable position, preferably with your feet on the ground or stretched out in front of you. Breathe deeply until you are feeling relaxed and yet alert. Now I want you to fast forward to a time in the future. You are ten years older. Everything and everyone around you is ten years older, too. You can't believe how quickly the years went by, but here you are anyway. You are with a close and trusted group of friends whom you haven't seen in ten years. You are all eager to know what everyone has been up to in the past decade. The topic turns to marriage. What do you say? Write down everything about your current marital status. Are you married? Are you separated or divorced? If you are married, are you happy? Are you fulfilled? What currently brings you the most joy? How is your sex life? What has surprised you the most about your current happiness? What stories will you tell about your happiest relationship moments these past few years?

Your friends are overjoyed for you. They remember that ten years ago you were hurt, unhappy, confused, and on the brink of divorce. They are amazed at your turnaround. They want to know how you got here. What did you do differently? Who did you associate with? How did you turn things around? You are smiling as you share your story. A lot has been packed into those years. You are overflowing with gratitude as you answer their questions. They can feel your joy and they want what you have. Tell them your story. Tell them about the ten years you've lived and conquered that are yet to come. Stop here and write the history of your future.

Don't read on until you've completed the last assignment. How did it feel? What did you look like ten years from now? How did it feel to be that happy and in a place you could hardly have imagined for yourself? Don't rush the process. Let it all sink in. You did this! You made this happen. You created exactly what you envisioned. You found the courage and discipline to create your dream. You have most likely heard the phrase, "If you can dream it, you can achieve it." It works because when you vividly envision a thing, your Reticular Activating System goes to work to make it happen for you.

What do you really want? What is your dream? You can have it if you know what you want.

For actual examples of Life Purpose statements join the Reclaim Your Life community at www.wivesatthecrossroads.com/getting started. It's free!

NOTES

CHAPTER FIVE:
TALKING TO THE WOMAN
IN THE MIRROR

It is when you lose sight of yourself,
that you lose your way.

—C. JoyBell C.

Who are you? What comes to mind when you first hear this question? Are you puzzled and unsure of what they are asking and hope you give the right response? Do you start by sharing your name and your vocation and credentials? Or do you pause and, with a knowing smile, offer a cheeky response, like *I am more than you could ever imagine?*

We all know the titles and roles we bear, but how often do you stop to think about the essence of who you are? Beyond being a wife, a mother, a daughter, a sister, an only child, a granddaughter, a friend, a community volunteer, a dance mom, a baseball team mom, a nurse, and all the other roles you play, who are you really?

If all those roles were stripped from you today, what would remain? Who are you at your core? This is not about who people think you are. From the moment we come into the world people are constantly trying to impose on us their ideas and perceptions of who they think we are or should be. The result is that many of us grow into adulthood never giving ourselves permission to define ourselves for ourselves. We spend a lifetime alternately conforming and rebelling against the images and expectations projected on us.

> **UNTIL YOU TAKE THE TIME TO DISCOVER AND OWN YOURSELF, YOU WILL NEVER ACHIEVE THE LIFE OF YOUR DREAMS.**

Until you take the time to discover and own yourself, you will never achieve the life of your dreams, because chances are your current dreams aren't even tied to the real essence of who you are and what you need. You may recall the movie *The Runaway Bride*, starring Julia Roberts. In the movie, Roberts' character, an otherwise sweet and loveable young woman, repeatedly bolts during her weddings, leaving groom after groom at the altar. She is not proud of her reputation and appears to really want to see her wedding through, but the end result was always the same. She couldn't commit. While I won't give the whole plot away, I can tell you that by the end of the movie, she finally realizes she had spent her whole life adapting to the men who were interested in her. She would present herself as a blank canvas upon which these men would inadvertently paint a picture of who they wanted her to be. She would, in turn, personify that picture until it was time to say "I do." In that moment, I think, her true self momentarily shows up, prompting her to literally break free and flee the scene. Although the men who courted her all seemed to be great guys, she was unable to create an authentic relationship and see it through until she took the time to search for and appreciate her true self.

Who are you? When everything is going just as you planned, who are you? When the whole world seems to be conspiring against you and the world is winning, who are you? What makes you come alive? What makes you shine? What makes you shrink back in fear? What occupies your thoughts? What childhood dreams have you buried? When do you feel most free? When are you overflowing with joy and peace? When are you in your darkest moments, and what takes and keeps you there? Self-discovery is simple, though it is not easy. Taking the time to peel back the layers of protection in which you have cloaked yourself is painful and isolating for most. You need time to be quiet and shut out the world to effectively hear a voice you've long ignored. Most people will not willingly make time for this level of introspection. It usually takes a crisis to force us to this place. Some never get there, but those who do and choose to do the work are transformed when they get to the core of who they really are.

A few years ago, I got a call from a number I didn't recognize, and, unlike my usual practice, I took the call. Her name was Samantha; she had gotten my number from a mutual friend. She needed someone to talk to and knew from my social media presence that I am a life coach. Although I usually charge for my services, the desperation in her voice persuaded me to hear her out.

For over an hour, Samantha poured out her heart, sharing stories she'd painstakingly hidden from the world. She described herself as the product of a rape. She's never found out who her dad is. Her mother was a prostitute, and, as a child, Samantha witnessed her getting roughed up by one man after another. Eventually, her mother was murdered, but not before little Samantha had been sexually molested by a few of her mother's johns.

After her mother's death, she was raised by an aunt who seemed to take great pleasure in reminding her every chance she got that her mother was a "good-for-nothing prostitute." Samantha is very physically attractive by any standard and was soon convinced that she was too stupid to get ahead except by using her body, but she was determined to prove the naysayers wrong. She wasn't her mother. She dated mature men in the hopes it would end in marriage. For a long time, it didn't, but eventually she did meet and marry who she thought was her knight in shining armor. He liked showing her off and she lived to please him. She got pregnant, added some pounds, and had the first of three children. She later found out that the day she gave birth to their first child, her husband had another woman in their matrimonial bed.

Samantha didn't have any career prospects. She had mostly worked low-paying jobs since her high school graduation. She wanted her children to have a stable childhood and so she committed to making her marriage work. She did whatever her husband required of her, and then some. But he no longer took her out, and if they happened to be in public together, he kept her at arm's length. He would make her look at herself naked in the mirror and point out all her flaws—the extra weight, the stretch marks, the sagging breasts. But verbal and emotional abuse soon weren't enough for him. He began to sexually debase her. Still she stayed. She wasn't her mother. She was a married woman, and too many people were watching and waiting for her to fail. She stayed even when he started hitting her. Her moment of awakening came in an ambulance with a paramedic.

She couldn't recall the details of what happened. One minute she was begging her husband to give her the night off because she was hurting from the beating she got the night before. She remembers him ripping her top and then everything went blank until she woke up in the ambulance. She later found out that her nine-year-old daughter had heard her scream and walked in on her dad strangling her mom, so she had run out to alert the neighbors, who called the police. Samantha's husband was gone by the time the police arrived.

The words of the paramedic still haunted her. He said, "Ma'am, I saw my pops kill my mom. You've got to save yourself or this man will kill you. Do it for your daughters, if you can't do it for you." She never found out the paramedic's name, but she will never forget his words.

She called me after she was released from the hospital. She was living in a shelter. Her children were with a relative. She was distraught and unsure of how to get back on her feet. She said, "This is a nightmare. I want my children safe and with me. I am not my mother." She wanted my help.

I worked with Samantha almost weekly for over twelve months. Today, she is in her own home with all her children. She's moved past survival and is now always brimming with ideas for future opportunities. She's taking classes for her next career while earning a living from her own small, home-based business. She's committed to being a great role model for her daughters and has changed her eating habits, consequently reaping great health benefits. It is amazing the odds she's overcome.

Where did our work start? It started where I am asking you to start. One of the most important questions Samantha had to answer for herself was "Who am I?" She had spent a lifetime living by "I am not my mother." She had spent no time figuring out who she was.

Through our work together, she began to unearth the treasure trove within her. She cried when she worked on the exercise to identify her strengths. First, the tears were of frustration because her sense of self was so muddied by what people had said and done to her. Then, the tears flowed out of amazement and gratitude as she began to acknowledge the creativity, beauty, and strength within herself.

One of the keys to her breakthrough came from an illustration that had been shared with me many years ago. A speaker took a hundred dollar bill and crumpled it up in her hand, then asked the audience what it was worth. Everyone yelled, "One hundred dollars!" Then she dropped the bill on the ground and stomped on it, and even asked some members of the audience to do the same. After all the stomping, she asked the audience what the bill was worth. They again screamed, "One hundred dollars!" Next, she brought out a trashcan and a bag of trash which included food scraps and a used baby diaper. She threw the bill in the trashcan and dumped the trash over it. She again asked the audience, "How much is that crumpled, dirty, smelly, slimy bill worth?" The audience jumped to their feet and screamed, "ONE HUNDRED DOLLARS!!!"

Your value is intrinsic. Your worth cannot be diminished by your experiences or what people have done to you. The only way you lose the benefit of your value is if you forget or never knew your value to begin with, and when you start to buy in to your undesirable circumstances. Knowing and celebrating who you are is one of the most empowering and liberating things you can do. It allows you to break free from the chains of others' judgments and actions. It nourishes and emboldens your dreams. It propels you beyond a life of mere survival to a life of meaning and excellence.

> YOUR VALUE IS INTRINSIC. YOUR WORTH CANNOT BE DIMINISHED BY YOUR EXPERIENCES OR WHAT PEOPLE HAVE DONE TO YOU.

I know this on a personal level. After surviving sexual molestation in my childhood, my self-esteem had taken quite a beating. Even as a child, though, I was determined to make something great of my life. I had to figure out who I was, and I knew that my self was not what had been done to me. A poem by Max Ehrmann, "Desiderata," became a tool for my rehabilitation and provided a map for my healing. It was on a plaque in our home for most of my childhood. I read the words repeatedly, even when I couldn't grasp the meaning in its entirety. I hope you draw the same (or more) encouragement from this poem as I always have:

Go placidly amid the noise and the haste,

and remember what peace there may be in silence.

As far as possible without surrender

be on good terms with all persons. Speak your truth quietly and clearly; and listen to others,

even the dull and the ignorant; they too have their story.

Avoid loud and aggressive persons, they are vexations to the spirit.

If you compare yourself with others, you may become vain and bitter;

for always there will be greater and lesser persons than yourself. Enjoy your achievements as well as your plans.

Keep interested in your own career, however humble; it is a real possession in the changing fortunes of time. Exercise caution in your business affairs;

for the world is full of trickery.

But let this not blind you to what virtue there is; Many persons strive for high ideals;

And everywhere life is full of heroism.

Be yourself.

Especially, do not feign affection. Neither be cynical about love;

for in the face of all aridity and disenchantment it is as perennial as the grass.

Take kindly the counsel of the years, gracefully surrendering the things of youth.

Nurture strength of spirit to shield you in sudden misfortune. But do not distress yourself with dark imaginings.

Many fears are born of fatigue and loneliness. Beyond a wholesome discipline,

be gentle with yourself.

You are a child of the universe, no less than the trees and the stars; you have a right to be here.

And whether or not it is clear to you,

no doubt the universe is unfolding as it should.

Therefore be at peace with God, whatever you conceive Him to be,

> *and whatever your labors and aspirations,*
> *in the noisy confusion of life keep peace with your soul.*

> *With all its sham, drudgery, and broken dreams, it is still a beautiful world.*
> *Be cheerful.*
> *Strive to be happy.*

* * *

Stephen Mitchell, in his interpretation of Chinese philosopher Lao Tzu's *Tao Te Ching*, astutely stated, "Much of our discontent stems from not consciously knowing and embracing who we are. When you are content to simply be yourself and don't compare or compete, everyone will respect you." Samantha courageously answered the question, "Who am I?" She says whenever fear starts to rise, whenever she feels overwhelmed or down on herself, she asks and answers that question. She faces the fear armed with the power of the truth of who she is, and the fear shrinks.

Strengths and Weaknesses

Businesses often utilize a tool called SWOT Analysis. It is a simple but useful framework for analyzing an organization's strengths and weaknesses, as well as the opportunities and threats it faces. Organizations employ this tool as a way of identifying and focusing on their strengths, minimizing threats, and taking the greatest possible advantage of opportunities available to them.

You and I, as individuals, can apply this same logic and tool to our lives and reap great dividends. Find a place where you can be quiet and uninterrupted for an hour or so. Get two pieces of paper. On the first page, write the heading *My Strengths*. On the second page, write *My Weaknesses*. On the first page, list at least ten strengths you possess. On the second page, write down ten weaknesses you've identified in yourself. Think back to your childhood. What comes naturally to you? What do you enjoy? What are your accomplishments? Where do you shine? What do people seek you out for? What's tripped you up in the past? Where have you disappointed yourself? What do you struggle with? What character trait have you been trying to change in yourself? Some clients have shared that while they can easily list ten or more weaknesses, they find it much more difficult to list their strengths.

One strategy you can employ to help you identify your strengths is to seek input from people who know you. Identify five to ten people, if you can, and ask them to share the positive characteristics and strengths they've seen in you. If you want to take it even further, ask them to share a time when they saw you playing to your strengths. Choose people from different aspects of your life: family, friends, coworkers, people from your place of worship, supervisors, your children, old classmates, neighbors, etc. Give them a time frame in which you need their response or most will procrastinate.

Once you receive the feedback, write down the common traits and themes and look for any patterns. Pay attention to the stories around the themes and the evidence people presented to back up their evaluation of your strengths. Note also what isn't said, or what you wish you did differently or better in the scenarios they presented. Add those strengths and any weaknesses you note to your list.

Next, look over both pages as objectively as you can, comparing your strengths to your weaknesses. Go back to the life purpose statement you created in chapter three. How can you build on your strengths to better live out your purpose? Look at the specific goals you identified for each area of your life; can you create a plan for more effectively achieving those goals based on your identified strengths? How have your weaknesses shown up in the past to derail your goals? How can you use your strengths to minimize or overcome your weaknesses? Do not gloss over this assignment. Don't just do it in your head. The clearer and more detailed your plan for achieving your goals is, the higher the likelihood of success. If you are unsure or vague about your strengths and how to apply them to your life, your results in your life will be vague and frustrating at best.

Those who are serious about reclaiming their life must get serious about identifying the tools and pathway that will most likely lead to their success. I am reminded of one of my favorite singers, Barbra Streisand. If you go to one of her concerts, you will see she's not trying to be a Tina Turner; she's not dancing across the entire stage, she's just singing. She's not trying to keep up with Cher; her clothes compliment her, but the focus is not on her outfits. She knows dancing and wearing revealing attire are not her strengths, but singing definitely is. She focuses on and maximizes her strength, and it has served her well for decades, with no end in sight. To create the marriage of your dreams, you must get clarity about who you are to help you identify the *how* of realizing your dream.

Vironika Tugaleva, author of *The Love Mindset* and *The Art of Talking to Yourself*, sums it up this way:

You are not who you think you are. You are not your fears, your thoughts, or your body. You are not your insecurities, your career, or your memories. You're not what you're criticized for and you're not what you're praised for. You are a boundless wealth of potential. You are everything that's ever been. Don't sell yourself short. Every sunset, every mountain, every river, every passionate crowd, every concert, every drop of rain— that's you. So go find yourself. Go find your strength, find your beauty, find your purpose. Stop crafting your mask. Stop hiding. Stop lying to yourself and letting people lie to you. You're not lacking in anything except awareness. Everything you've ever wanted is already there, awaiting your attention, awaiting your time.

If you are not ready to do this work now, you are lying to yourself about wanting what you say you want. It is as true in our lives as it is in nature: what you sow is what you reap, if it is sown with wisdom. A rice farmer doesn't buy land in a desert and hope they can coax rice plants out of the arid soil. They buy land in an area that lends itself to the best use of their talents. The same applies to you. Know your purpose. Set your goals according to your purpose. Identify your strengths and apply them. Get creative about minimizing your weaknesses. Believe in yourself. Face your fears. Do this over and over again and you will be well on your way to reclaiming your life.

Visit www.wivesatthecrossroads.com/worksheets to download a SWOT analysis worksheet.

NOTES

CHAPTER SIX:
CHOOSE TO LEAD YOURSELF

Take your life in your own hands, and what happens?
A terrible thing: no one to blame.

—Erica Jong

There's a curious thing I've observed, even amongst the most accomplished of women: many of us abdicate our power to create
the lives we really want and instead throw ourselves headfirst into
being what everyone else says we should be. This means that we
often stop communicating our needs and expectations, and trade
our hopes for companionship and intimacy with our spouse for
superwoman capes.

The problem with the superwoman, supermom syndrome is
three-fold. First of all, you train your spouse and everyone around
you to believe that you really can do it all on your own, and they
are all too happy to let you do just that, no matter what it costs you.
Secondly, it repels intimacy because your act of invincibility con-
vinces others you really don't need them. Thirdly, your resentment

at your sacrifices and lack of support builds and either you burn out or you literally blow up. I had a cape, too. I wore it with much pride. It took me a while, but one day I just decided to burn that cape. I was exhausted from trying to be all things to all people—the ideal wife and mother, dutiful daughter and daughter-in-law, worker, dependable church member, and so on.

> I WAS EXHAUSTED FROM TRYING TO BE ALL THINGS TO ALL PEOPLE—THE IDEAL WIFE AND MOTHER, DUTIFUL DAUGHTER AND DAUGHTER-IN-LAW, WORKER, DEPENDABLE CHURCH MEMBER, AND SO ON.

What I had been doing was not getting me where I wanted to be. It was time for change, and the change had to start with me. It was time to show up differently in my own life. I decided to LEAD myself. As a leader, I determined that the two most important areas of focus for me were communication and self-care. As John C. Maxwell says, "A leader is one who knows the way, goes the way, and shows the way." As a mother, it was imperative for me to figure out how to create the life I imagined I would live so that I can model for my sons and daughters how to live their lives magnificently. To LEAD myself, I committed to loving myself, educating myself, acting on my insights, and distinguishing myself in everything I do.

Love Yourself

What does it mean to love yourself? We spend so much time yearning for others to love us. But what about self-love? It's noteworthy that even the Bible teaches that self-love is paramount, as we are encouraged to love our neighbors as we love ourselves. While we tend to put all our energy and focus on loving others, those actions are draining if they do not emanate from a place of self-love. How do you currently love yourself? What does that love look, sound, smell, taste, and feel like? Take the time to write down your answers. You deserve to know how you want to be loved, and your first clues lie in how you express that love to yourself.

My self-love smells like lavender, jasmine, lilies, and the perfume Beautiful. Any of those aromas has the power to ease my stress and transport me to a place of tranquility and contentment. My self-love feels like a gentle breeze, the heat of the sun on the back of my neck as I tend my garden, the ache of my muscles after a workout. My self-love sounds like Randy Crawford singing "Everything Must Change," Diana Ross declaring her independence in "It's My Turn," and Lionel Richie assuring me that I am "Once, Twice, Three Times a Lady." My self-love also sounds like me crying in gratitude, telling myself I am beautiful, capable, and worthy of all my dreams. My self-love looks like a strong and fit body, a garden full of beautiful flowers and vegetables, a bookcase weighed down with books. My self-love tastes like a serving of warm, freshly baked apple pie with a dollop of vanilla ice cream, several sips of cool water on a hot day, and a swig of freshly tapped palm wine. My self-love feels, sounds, tastes, looks, and smells so good to me.

Look over your responses. How do you feel? Did you smile as you wrote them? Did you cry? Were you wistful as you noted how seldom you carve out time to love yourself? What do your answers tell you about how you love yourself? Is your self-love tied to what others do or how they respond to you? Is it dependent on other people? Does it take a fortune for you to express love to yourself, or can you be loving to yourself all day long regardless of your circumstances?

Silvia sought me out after working with a counselor for years. She didn't feel she had made much headway regarding her issues. She had been blindsided by a divorce four years earlier. She was unhappy with her personal life, her job, and her career prospects. She felt unloved and unlovable. In addition to seeing a counselor, her physician had also put her on some antidepressants, but nothing seemed to lift the cloud in her head. As we talked, I realized that Silvia was obsessively focused on things beyond her control. So, I suggested an assignment which I hoped would enable her to look within. I asked Silvia to do one loving thing for herself every day for sixty-six days.

First she was irritated by the request, then she was perplexed. "How am I supposed to show love to myself?" she asked.

"That's for you to figure out," I said. She thought it was a stupid idea and a waste of her time. I asked her to indulge me for just three days.

I called Silvia on the fourth day. Initially, I thought I must have called the wrong number. The person who answered the phone was incoherent. All I could make out were loud, gasping sobs, the kind where you can't catch your breath and you probably have snot running down your face. Finally, I heard her say, "How did I get here?" She wasn't looking for nor did she need a response from me, so I remained quiet.

Silvia went on to share how hard the last three days had been for her. She started off irritated by the assignment. Her irritation soon turned to frustration because all her ideas on how to show herself love involved other people, and each person she called had been unavailable. Frustration gave way to despair when it dawned on her that she had forgotten how to love herself. I was in awe of her willingness to be so vulnerable. How many times have you or I shied away from the truth about ourselves because we lacked the courage to face it? That willingness to be vulnerable is the key to intimacy with oneself and with anyone else. As long as we feel the need to keep our masks and capes on, we insulate ourselves from authentic love.

With her new awareness, Silvia discovered that she was well acquainted with abusing herself. She berated herself all day in her head. She ate junk food most of the time and had to admit she was on her way to becoming an alcoholic (her words, not mine). She was surprised to find out it probably wasn't the best idea to mix alcohol with her medications. She hated her own company. She hated to hear herself speak because her voice grated on her ears. Finally, she asked, "How could anyone love me when I despise myself?"

What does your self-care look like?

But Silvia is no quitter. As heartbreaking as it was for her to admit her self-loathing despite all her accomplishments, she was determined to get to the root of it all and be intentional about writing the next chapters of her life. She focused on figuring out how to nurture her spirit and her physical body. She enrolled in a Mindfulness course and began to reprogram her mind with daily affirmations of the life she desired and the love she deserved. She identified four habits she wanted to embody over the next twelve months, focusing on each habit for three months, at which time it would become part of her daily routine and she could move to the next. One of her new habits is to spend five minutes every morning and evening affirming herself. That may sound weird to you, but our self-talk plays a significant role in how we see ourselves, and that impacts our choices. In twelve months, she had successfully overridden four bad habits by adopting four new habits that served her future. Her doctor was able to take her off the antidepressants. Silvia had decided to LEAD herself, and she started with loving herself exactly as she was, even as she worked on the areas where she desired growth. Today, Silvia is excited about the new her and is confident of the love she will eventually attract.

How can you love you? What does self-care look like in your life? How will you speak to yourself? How will you silence the negativity around you? LEAD yourself by intentionally choosing to demonstrate your love and gratitude to yourself.

Educate Yourself

Educating myself is by far the best investment I have made in my life. To LEAD yourself, you must commit to educating yourself, not because it is required of you, but because you require it of yourself. The better the understanding you have of yourself and the more willing you are to build on your strengths by adding to your knowledge base, the better you position yourself to create the life of your dreams.

Go back to your life purpose statement and review your goals, strengths, and weaknesses. What do you want out of life? What is keeping you from living your dream life? What issues keep recurring in your life? What lessons are your results trying to teach you? Pay attention and make a list of where you want to see improvement in your life.

Have financial woes plagued you no matter how much you earn? Educate yourself on finances. Is your health less than optimal? Educate yourself on what needs to change. What patterns do you see in your work? Are there courses or certifications you need to pursue to better position yourself for success? Do your relationships tend to take a predictable course? How do you typically deal with conflict? What is the default setting on your communication style? In other words, when you are tired or stressed, how well do you communicate?

> ### WHAT IS THE DEFAULT SETTING ON YOUR COMMUNICATION STYLE?

Although the importance of effective communication is stressed in the workplace, most of us in our day-to-day lives end up emulating what we saw around us as children. If your mother was a yeller, there is an excellent chance you will be a yeller, too. If your parents raised their voices at each other whenever there was a disagreement, or perhaps even walked out on each other when things got rough, you will most likely exhibit the same tendencies. Adults model what they learned as children.

Most people tend not to evaluate their communication style until there is a problem, and sometimes they still never get around to addressing their communication deficiencies, because they are either wired to believe that the problem lies with the other person or simply unmotivated to make what they consider a tough change. To LEAD yourself, it is worthwhile to evaluate and work on improving your communication skills; regardless of whether your marriage works out or not, great communication skills will enhance your life in so many ways. Though this chapter is not primarily meant to cover effective interpersonal communication, I will address a few communication *dos* and *don'ts* that I cover in my webinars on the topic. Improving your communication skills is critical to the success of any marriage and for a successful life.

Listening Skills

Moving forward, pay attention to your listening skills. Do you tend to hear people out, or are you the type to interrupt, finish other people's sentences, or assume that, as you already know what point they are about to make, you therefore do not have to hear from them? Do you listen with your whole being, or are you typically distracted or multitasking as others talk with you? Do you abruptly change the topic during a conversation? These are all ways we diminish people and convey that we are disinterested in whatever they have to share. When you shut a person down enough times, you shut down any chance of effective communication with that person. *Do* listen attentively to people.

R-E-S-P-E-C-T

How often have you been in a conversation that became disrespect-ful? Were you the one doing the disrespecting or the one being dis-respected? If you've ever been on the receiving end, how did it make you feel? Being disrespected often hits us in our guts and sends our senses spinning. Our blood pressure rises as we contemplate our re-sponse. Very little good ever comes out of a conversation where one party feels disrespected. Over time, the person on the receiving end will disengage. *Don't* disrespect others. *Do* set good boundaries so people know what is unacceptable to you and why. As you LEAD yourself, be sure to determine and communicate your boundaries. This, too, is a form of self-love.

Communicate on the Right Level

One of the most frustrating types of conversation to hold is with someone who chooses to throw facts at you when you are focused on heart issues, or a person who attempts to manipulate you with their emotions when you appropriately present facts. There are essentially two levels of communication: the heart level and the head level. At the heart level, a person is focused on their emotions. They are tuned in to their joy, anger, pain, bliss, or disappointment. In that moment, the last thing they want to hear are cold, hard facts or statistics. If you tend to be a problem solver, you may gloss over another's need to communicate with you at the heart level and move immediately to communicating on a head level, which sends a message that you are insensitive or uncaring, and vice versa. *Do* educate yourself to clue in to what level of communication is most effective in any situation.

Timing Is Everything

Sometimes, what causes conflict is not what you say, but when you say it. *Do* pay attention to the timing of your communication. It will affect your outcomes.

Speak Up

It is safe to assume that most people are not psychics. Therefore, it is important that, as you LEAD yourself, you get comfortable speaking your mind confidently. Many misunderstandings can be avoided if both parties have the courage and feel comfortable enough to speak their true minds, as opposed to hoping or expecting one person to "read the tea leaves" and know what's on the other person's mind. Most of the times when I have silenced my voice have led to regrettable circumstances. *Do* speak up, and clearly. *Do* create an environment that encourages others to speak frankly with you.

Look for the Good

Don't immediately jump to the worst conclusions about people. If there are multiple meanings to what they say, err on the side of the most favorable interpretation.

Do give people the benefit of the doubt.

Nonverbal Communication

For the most part, I follow the advice that if you have nothing positive to say, you should be quiet. Unfortunately, I often forget to remind my face of that. There have been numerous conversations with my spouse where I successfully stopped myself from speaking unhelpful thoughts, only to have my facial expressions, body language, gestures, or eyes tell the whole story anyway. This was counterproductive to effectively communicating with my husband, and these kinds of missteps exact a heavy price on any relationship. *Do* monitor your nonverbal communication. The best way to do that is to keep your thought process open and nonjudgmental.

Emotional Awareness

In my coaching program, I spend a significant amount of time on emotional awareness and mastery. An essential part of LEADing yourself is to be the mistress of your own emotions, rather than being led by your emotions. People led by their emotions tend to be impulsive and irrational, creating chaos wherever they go. Mastering your emotions is key to being able to turn your dreams into reality. *Don't* be a slave to your emotions.

Love Language

Do you know your love language? Do you know the love language of your spouse? I recall my first visit to Brazil. I didn't speak any Portuguese and had neglected to bring any tools that could aid me in communicating with non-English speakers. When I attempted to order dinner for my family waiting for me in the hotel room, it soon became very clear that the communication barrier between me and the food vendor could lead to my whole family starving. After what seemed like an eternity, the food was ordered. I was exhausted from the ordeal and I am sure she felt the same way.

The same miscommunication occurs in marriage and in other relationships. When two people are speaking differing languages, they are making perfect sense to themselves but not to each other.

Frustration mounts and, depending on their level of awareness, resentment builds. Resentment in a marriage is like seawater to metal. It isn't immediately obvious, but over time it will eat away at that metal until there is nothing left but rust.

The 5 Love Languages: The Secret to Love That Lasts by Gary Chapman outlines five ways to express and experience love: gift giving, quality time, words of affirmation, acts of service (devotion), and physical touch. To LEAD yourself is to know and understand your love language and to recognize and effectively communicate in the love languages of others. The better you are at bridging communication gaps, the more likely it is for you to create your dream life. *Do* become proficient at all the love languages.

Conflict Management

Conflict is not only inevitable, but it can also be beneficial when handled properly. To LEAD yourself, you must be cognizant of your default setting for handling conflict. Do you avoid conflict? Do you just ignore it and hope it will resolve itself? Do you create conflict? Do you face it head on with your focus on a mutual resolution? How have you dealt with conflict in your marriage? To LEAD yourself is to educate yourself on more effective ways to conflict resolution.

Rather than fleeing, shutting down, or blowing up, *do* choose to engage the other person in dialogue. Validate them by focusing on behavior and events, not on attacking their personalities. Choose to listen and identify points of agreement and disagreement. Ascertain what the real conflict is and commit to a plan to work on it. The better you become at dealing with conflict, the less stress and more impact you will have in your life and marriage.

Act on Your Insights

Leaders act. Don't just dream about the life you hope you can live. Don't just wish that your marriage was more loving or nurturing. Don't just pray that things change for the better for you. Remember the exercise you did on the future of the history of your marriage? Reread what you wrote and ask yourself: "What actions can I begin to employ right now to create my dream marriage?"

Well-meaning people fail to follow through on their plans for a variety of reasons. They might lack confidence in themselves and their abilities. Rather than trying and not initially succeeding, they don't try at all. Some people are plagued by perfectionism (also known as being control freaks); if they can't guarantee the outcome, they talk themselves out of taking action. Some people are professional procrastinators. They are experts at putting things off until tomorrow, but tomorrow either never comes or comes too late. Others are simply lazy. They are unmotivated to get going, even for their own good.

Review your goals, review the list of skills you've determined you need to live out your life purpose, and review your responses on the Eneli Abundant Life Scale. Create a game plan for acting on your goals. What can you start doing now to minimize the frustration in your marriage and life? Here's a practical idea: Create a list of the things you've identified that need to change. Separate the ones where you can take unilateral action from those where the cooperation of your spouse is desired. Find a good time to discuss these action items with your spouse and agree on roles and responsibilities. Your list may include: household finances, meal planning and grocery shopping, car maintenance, cooking, laundry, children's activities and schoolwork, house cleaning, spiritual development, etc. Finally, learn to delegate.

You may have heard of the Pareto principle. For the most part, the principle states that a small percentage of all you do creates the majority of the success you achieve. Successful people focus in on what really brings about the most success in their lives and then delegate everything else. If hiring a maid service will eliminate the constant bickering between you and your spouse regarding household chores, hire a service. If eating out a couple of nights a week will free up your time and energy for an active sex life with your spouse, for crying out loud, eat out. Don't just think about what may be possible, act to make it reality.

> ## PATRICIA IS MISERABLY MARRIED. SHE'S BECOME A PRO AT MASKING HER PAIN.

By her own admission, Patricia is miserably married. She's become a pro at masking her pain, but when the mask is down, Patricia's hopelessness is etched into every line on her face and her despair weighs heavily on her words.

Patricia is the pride and joy of her parents. She was a good student. Her parents could always count on her to make good choices. She lived a sheltered life that consisted of school, home, and church. She describes her parents' marriage as stable. Her mother supported her father's career and he made most of the decisions in their home. While Patricia was in college, her father passed away. As a result, the family became strained financially, and she had to figure out how to fend for herself and help her mother.

Patricia got married at age twenty-three. It seemed the right thing to do, and she unconsciously expected her husband to lift the financial burden off her family. Her mother was overjoyed at the marriage and quickly assigned to her son-in-law all the deference her husband had enjoyed.

But things weren't going so great for Patricia. Her husband took pleasure in pointing out her flaws and belittling her. This continued even after their children became old enough to understand what was going on. She tried to get advice from her mother, but her mother only reinforced that she was at fault for not adequately catering to her husband's needs.

Patricia threw herself into excelling in her workplace and in parenting her children. She endured her husband's disrespect and they spent as little time as they could together. This continued for years. Patricia built a reputation as a great leader in her workplace, where she enjoyed great respect, growing influence, and a significant paycheck. She was given all the tougher cases because everyone knew if anyone could turn things around, Patricia could.

However, it was a much different story at home. Patricia could diagnose the issues in her marriage with the skill of a seasoned marriage counselor. But that's as far as she would go. She would identify the issues, ruminate on how awful and unsupportive her husband is, and complain about the endless arguments and how intensely lonely she was in her marriage, but she would take no action.

As we talked, Patricia admitted that as a child, she lost respect for her mother because of her mother's willingness to be dominated by her father. She is upset with herself for, as strong and accomplished as she is, she still ended up repeating the same patterns in her own marriage. She knows things must change before she loses her mind, but the amount of effort she thinks is required for any change and the uncertainty of how her actions will impact her and her children keep her immobilized. But inaction is still a form of action and carries its own consequences. She began to experience frequent headaches.

Patricia wanted help. I think she secretly hoped I had a magic wand that she could just wave to make everything better instantly. Over the course of a few months, Patricia tapped into the magic within. She had it all along and only needed support to face the hurdles in her personal life. Patricia has not decided if she will leave her marriage or not, but she no longer sees herself as a victim condemned to a lifetime of misery. For now, she has successfully established boundaries in her marriage. She is taking ownership of her life—finances, communication style, and health—and is engaging in activities outside of home, work, and church for the first time as a married woman. She's optimistic about her future. Patricia had finally decided to LEAD herself.

Leaders take action. Women have become more confident leading in the workplace, now it is time to lead ourselves in a way that empowers us and transforms our lives positively. Give yourself permission to show up boldly in your own life. Taking action may feel risky, but the bigger risk is to do nothing. Would you rather get behind the wheel of a car or be a passenger in a moving car with no driver?

Distinguish Yourself

I am so excited about helping women turn this corner in their lives, to recognize that it is not just okay, it is desirable to be distinguished. We should aim to be our very best, unapologetically. Sheryl Sandberg's book *Lean In: Women, Work, and the Will to Lead* resonated with so many women in part because many of us can admit that we have, on too many occasions, ceded our power and abandoned our dreams. And to what end?

I remember a painful yet empowering conversation I had with my now eighteen-year-old son. He called me a hypocrite, and it stung because I pride myself on being a person of integrity and living what I preach. He said, "Mom, you are so talented. Every day, you are empowering us to set and reach our goals. You are coaching others to be excellent, but you put your dreams on hold for us. Why haven't you finished your book? What about your dreams?" I fought back my tears. I was annoyed that he would dare to call me a hypocrite, a word I so reviled. I wanted to argue him down to show how my sacrifices had helped set him up for the bright future he and his siblings have, but I didn't. I didn't fight back because there was too much truth in what he had said. Yes, I am quite accomplished, but I also know all too well the dreams lying dormant between the pages of the journals I've accumulated over the years. I know it is time to go to another level. When you and I play small, we never, ever, ever win. Mediocrity serves neither us nor anyone else, as a matter of fact. To LEAD is to choose to distinguish yourself.

What are some synonyms for distinguished? Outstanding, acclaimed, brilliant, dignified, eminent, esteemed, great, honored, illustrious, noble, notable, remarkable, reputable, venerable, extraordinary. Think back to your life purpose statement; how can you possibly live out that purpose without committing to being excellent in every area of your life? Can you envision how choosing to be extraordinary will propel you to greater heights of success and enable you to powerfully influence issues that are important to you? Think of all the areas of your life currently causing you pain. What if you experienced even a 10 percent improvement in any of those areas? What if you saw a 10 percent improvement each year in every area of your life for the next five years? What would that look like for you? What would it feel like?

To LEAD yourself is to choose to distinguish yourself. It is stepping up and playing big even though the spotlight leaves you more vulnerable to attacks. As José Ortega y Gasset noted, "We distinguish the excellent man from the common man by saying that the former is the one who makes great demands on himself, and the latter who makes no demands on himself."

I want every woman in the world to internalize the idea of distinguishing herself, of making her life count, of living and leaving a legacy. How do you make this possible in your life? As famed singer, actress, and performer Janet Jackson famously said, "Dreams can become a reality when we possess a vision that is characterized by the willingness to work hard, a desire for excellence, and a belief in our right and our responsibility to be equal members of society." If you've followed the directives in this book so far, you have already assembled most of the tools you need. You have a clear vision of what you want. You've taken inventory of your strengths and weaknesses. You have a plan for where you want to go. All you need now is the willingness to work hard, a desire for excellence, and a mindset that won't let you quit. LEAD yourself by distinguishing yourself.

Download a worksheet on allocation of home chores at www. wivesatthecrossroads/worksheets.

NOTES

CHAPTER SEVEN: UNLEASH YOUR SEXUAL BEING— SEX AND INTIMACY MATTER

*He reaches for my body and I let him, but all the while
I am wishing he would reach for my soul.*

—Aya Fubara Eneli

DEBRA: We are putting the house on the market.

ME: Why is that?

DEBRA: We are thinking of going on a trial separation.

ME: What do you think about that?

DEBRA: I think he is seeing someone else. I never thought it would come to this, but here we are.

ME: How do you feel about that?

DEBRA: I guess I should have seen it coming.

ME: Why? Did you?

DEBRA: We haven't had sex in over two years. I can't remember the last time we even kissed.

ME: Was that by mutual agreement?

DEBRA: Not really. We never talk about it. It's just how things are. I don't think we knew how to talk about it and now it is too late. I can't even imagine him touching me.

ME: If you could change things, what would you change?

DEBRA: Honestly? Nothing. I've never enjoyed sex and I don't miss it.

ME: How about intimacy? Touch?

DEBRA: How about it?

ME: Have you heard of the Failure to Thrive syndrome in babies?

DEBRA: No.

ME: I'll give you the condensed version. The book *Born for Love* chronicles how over a third of all infants housed in orphanages die and over half of them present with significant mental problems. Research shows that the lack of human touch and affection is the cause. The book says: "Basically, they die from lack of love. When an infant falls below the threshold of physical affection needed to stimulate the production of growth hormone and the immune system, his [or her] body starts shutting down."

DEBRA: Yep, my body and mind shut down a long time ago.

ME: When?

DEBRA: When I was raped as a child.

What Roles Do Intimacy and Sex Really Play in a Marriage?

While I could quote research findings and expert opinions in response to this question, what really matters is what's important to you and your husband. Why did you both get married? Were sex and intimacy an understood part of what you both expected in your marriage? What is your vision for your marriage? What is his vision for your marriage? Are you both seeking the same things from your union? Are you both happy with your current level of sexual activity and intimacy? Have you ever had an open conversation about sex—his needs, your needs, his likes, your likes, his fears, your fears? When was your last open, nonjudgmental conversation on your mutual sexual and intimacy needs with your spouse?

Over the years, I have come to learn that most men are deeply concerned about their ability to perform sexually. This concern seems to increase as men get older, particularly if there are any health challenges like diabetes, hypertension, depression, and other chronic medical problems.

> **PERHAPS EVEN MORE IMPORTANT THAN SEX IS THE ROLE INTIMACY PLAYS IN THE QUALITY OF A MARRIAGE.**

Generally speaking, sex is one aspect of your relationship as husband and wife that should differentiate it from all other relationships you may have. While there are other ways to achieve closeness, sex is an important means of expressing romantic love and strengthening marital bonds. Many couples indicate that it helps them draw closer to each other emotionally. Furthermore, it adds fun and levity to their relationship, and frequent sexual intercourse causes them to be kinder to one another. Fulfilling each other's sexual needs makes them less vulnerable to interest from others and happier in their relationships.

Perhaps even more important than sex is the role intimacy plays in the quality of a marriage. Dr. Barton Goldsmith, in an article for *Psychology Today*, defined intimacy as "an exchange of tender energy between two people who love each other deeply." Intimacy can be expressed anywhere and is key to strengthening the bond between two people. Intimacy can be achieved in a myriad of ways. It is gently brushing against your spouse as you do your chores. It is a sweet kiss to the forehead. It shows up as an arm draped across the shoulders of your spouse. It is any specific attempt at speaking your spouse's love language. Intimacy can transform a person's mood in a heartbeat. Intimacy does not have to be sexual.

But before you can address the state of your marriage in terms of sex and intimacy, it behooves you to honestly assess your feelings about sex and intimacy. Do you like sex? Why? Is it important to you to enjoy intimacy? How do you define intimacy? How do you express it and how do you receive it? Do you know what you like sexually? Have you ever communicated your sexual likes or dislikes with your spouse? Do you know your sexual boundaries? Regardless of whether you ultimately rebuild or leave your marriage, you still need to come to terms with your mindset and feelings regarding sex, sexual pleasure, and intimacy. You deserve to show up fully present in your life. Married couples owe it to each other to have these conversations so they can make the most of their marriages.

Unfortunately, many of us go into marriage completely unprepared to have these conversations. To exacerbate matters, some of us may even have had previous sexual experiences that have negatively impacted us. For women who may want to further explore the roadblocks in this area in their lives, I strongly encourage you to consider Shannon Ethridge's Woman at the Well Intensive Workshop. You can get more information on the transformative work she does in this area at www.shannonethridge.com/wowintensive/.

Why Sex?

Sex is good for you! Sex with a person you love and who loves you back is literally heaven on earth. It is my joy to share the information in this chapter with you because this is an area I struggled with for many years. And because I struggled with it, it affected my marriage and my overall quality of life. When I told my husband almost twenty years ago that I didn't just want to be married for marriage's sake, that I wanted a loving, passionate, fulfilling marriage, I meant every word. The challenge was how to get from where I was to where I wanted to be. How was I supposed to heal from the invisible scars of childhood sexual molestation? How was I supposed to give up my need to be in control?

> **THE PROBLEM IS WE WANT TO LOVE AND BE LOVED, BUT WE ALSO WANT TO KEEP CONTROL. YET, LOVE IS SURRENDERING THE DESIRE TO CONTROL THE OTHER PERSON AND GIVING UP THE FEAR OF BEING CONTROLLED.**

I may not know the specifics of your story, but I have spent the last eighteen years listening to women with all kinds of sexual issues and hang-ups. I had a client who had been married for twenty-five years and had never been intimate with her husband with the lights on. Some women get very embarrassed about their breasts, especially after nursing or as they start to lose firmness. Bombarded by images of supposedly perfect women, some wives are overcome by their perceived inadequacies. I have coached wives who have never experienced an orgasm. They describe scenes like the one in the movie *Waiting to Exhale*, where the male character grunted and puffed on top of Whitney Houston's character for all of thirty seconds before climaxing and promptly falling into deep sleep, complete with loud snoring. What a turn off!

Christian girls, and others from very conservative upbringings, have the additional issue of overcoming the voices in their heads, the years of indoctrination on what is acceptable sexually and what isn't. Some have been taught that sex is just for the pleasure of the man—good girls shouldn't enjoy sex—or that sex should be just for the purpose of procreation. One lady I talked to described swallowing the vomit in her mouth as she allowed her spouse to do things she found embarrassing and distasteful. She had been raised to please her husband at all costs.

Then there are those women whose spouses have cheated on them. They are supposed to quickly forgive and forget and carry on like the betrayal never occurred. We have yet another group of wives whose husbands are addicted to pornography. Their husbands derive more sexual satisfaction from other women and from computer images. I recall a young and physically attractive wife in her thirties who was completely crushed because her husband had no interest in having sex with her. She felt unwanted, rejected, and completely detached from him. There are, of course, women who care nothing for sex with their spouse (or anyone else, as a matter of fact) and would prefer to coexist with their husbands as roommates. Health complications, as well as medications and their side effects, can also take their toll on sex in marriage.

Without a doubt, the busyness of our modern lives and schedules can significantly impact the quality and frequency of sex. Add children to that equation, and catching up on sleep or meeting the needs of the children becomes a priority over sex and even intimacy with your spouse. If a couple has experienced infertility, sex may cease to be an act of love and more of just a means to an end. Some women suffer through post-partum depression, which negatively affects every area of their life, including their libido. Many people use sex to manipulate and control their spouse. They withhold affection and sex as a means of punishment or use it as a reward. Such acts ensure that the controlling spouse can never be truly vulnerable in their marriage. Vulnerability is essential to cultivate intimacy and to go beyond just the physical act of sex. The issues abound. Should we care? What roles do intimacy and sex really play in a marriage? How have intimacy and sex factored into the current state of your marriage?

Can Sex Improve Your Health?

Sex doesn't just feel good, there's much evidence that it is also good for our health under the right circumstances. There is a plethora of scientifically backed values to being sexually active. Monogamous sex with your husband eliminates the disease risk of sex and allows you to enjoy all the advantages. Some of the benefits include the following:

Reduced Risk of Fatal Heart Attacks

Did you know that heart disease is the number one killer of women? According to the *Journal of Epidemiology and Community Health*, having sex at least twice a week can reduce the risk of fatal heart attacks by 50 percent. That's huge!

Stronger Immune System

How can having sex twice or more a week keep the cold and flu away? Researchers at Wilkes University in Pennsylvania report that having sex frequently boosts the immune system. In an article in *Women's Health Magazine*, Debby Herbenick, MD, explained that sex has the effect of increasing levels of IgA, or immunoglobulin A. Apparently, IgA increases resistance to a variety of illnesses.

Weight Loss

You can burn as much as 75–150 calories per half hour of sex, according to Desmond Ebanks, MD, founder and medical director of Alternity Healthcare in West Hartford, Connecticut. Have more sex with your spouse and control your weight in the process.

Lowers Blood Pressure

Joseph J. Pinzone, MD, CEO and medical director of AMAI Medical and Wellness, says that "one landmark study found that sexual intercourse specifically (not masturbation) lowered systolic blood pressure." Your systolic blood pressure is the first number on your blood pressure test.

Cures Headaches and Other Pains

According to Barry R. Komisaruk, Rutgers University professor, if you have a headache, an orgasm will work just as well or better than an aspirin. He states, "We've found that vaginal stimulation can block chronic back and leg pain, and many women have told us that genital self-stimulation can reduce menstrual cramps, arthritic pain, and in some cases even headache."

Sex also improves sleep and eases stress. My husband had tried to explain this to me for years. In my childbearing and nursing years, sex at the end of an exhausting day was the last on my list of things I wanted to do. While I was focused on getting some rest before the next baby feeding, my husband wanted to have sex and was emphatic it relaxed him and helped him sleep. Most nights, that argument held no sway with me. Dr. Sheenie Ambardar, a psychiatrist, agrees with my husband: "After orgasm, the hormone prolactin is released, which is responsible for the feelings of relaxation and sleepiness."

There are many more health benefits to engaging in frequent sex with a trusted partner; take advantage of this natural healer.

To Thy Own Self Be True

As with marriage itself, which should be built on mutual love and respect, your sex life shouldn't be one that is imposed upon you. Unfortunately, sex tends not to be a topic couples discuss at length prior to marriage. Many are too inhibited, naïve, or afraid of being judged and possibly rejected. Couples often begin a marriage with differing ideas of what their sex life will be like. If you haven't talked with your spouse about your sexual satisfaction and expectations for your marriage, now is a great time. Be sure to listen carefully and without judgment. Do the work to come to some understanding about what you both want out of your marriage.

With all the ideas we get from society on how to have a great sex life, it is important that sex in your marriage edifies you and builds you up as opposed to leaving you feeling used and abused. Often, one spouse may have some more "adventurous" ideas of what would spice up their sex life. Here are some guidelines on what sex should be.

SEX SHOULD BE CONSENSUAL AND AN EXPRESSION OF LOVE.

Sex should be consensual and an expression of love. It is debilitating to a woman and her marriage when she feels forced to have sex with her spouse. I remember a frantic call from a client years ago. She said, "I think I was just raped. Is that legal? Can my own husband rape me?" They had been having some marital difficulties, which had affected their sex life. On this day, he tried to grab and kiss her, and when she rebuffed his advances, he pinned her on the bed and penetrated her anyway. Many cultures reject the idea that a rape can occur between husband and wife. Even in the US, state laws differ on this issue, and like with other forms of rape, marital rape is underreported. This client did not report her rape. She eventually divorced her husband.

Sex should be intimate. It should never be used as a weapon or withheld as punishment, or feel forced or pressured. Rather than shaming your spouse into having sex or making them feel guilty about their lack of interest or desire, a better approach for the health of the relationship is to explore how to support your spouse so both your sexual needs are met. Dr. Kevin Leman's bestselling book *Sex Begins in the Kitchen* has great insights to help couples build intimacy and increase sexual interest all day, as opposed to right before one spouse initiates sex.

Sex should be a natural drive and never a compulsion. Sex addiction and other addictions that can affect sexual relations abound. If you sense you or your spouse has an issue in this area, seek professional help immediately.

Sex should be respectful and empowering and should enhance self-esteem and confidence. It should not include objects or activities that you are uncomfortable including or using. It should never be painful unless pain is expressly part of the agreed-upon enjoyment. Sex should never include acts that you feel denigrate you.

It Is All About You

Barring any physical limitations, sexual pleasure and intimacy begins in the mind. As with most things in life, your focus determines your outcome. Examine your childhood impressions and teachings about marriage, love, and sex. What lessons did you learn formally and informally about sex? What did you learn about your role as a woman as it pertains to sex? What did your parents model for you? Were you raised in a home where your parents openly displayed their affection for and attraction to each other?

> ## WHAT DO YOU BELIEVE TO BE TRUE ABOUT SEX? ARE YOUR BELIEFS POSITIVE, NEGATIVE, OR INDIFFERENT?

What rules of sexual engagement have you adopted for yourself? Can good women desire sex? Do good mothers initiate sex? Should women become asexual once they have children or reach a certain age? What conditions must you have to "feel" like having sex? Do you know your body? How comfortable are you with your body, sexuality, and sensuality? What do you believe to be true about sex? Are your beliefs positive, negative or indifferent? Review your response to the History of Your Future Marriage exercise. Did you include anything about your sex life? Why? Don't just gloss over these questions. The time you take to answer these questions may be one of the best investments you make in yourself and in your marriage.

One of the biggest gifts I have given myself, and by default my husband, is to reclaim my sexual power. My earliest recollection of sex is when I was about five years old. An adult male cousin held me up against a wall and was humping on me and making animal noises. I was confused and terrified. It happened so quickly. He put me down and told me not to tell anyone. He was one of my caregivers when my parents were at work. Without realizing it, that experience and others etched a thought in my mind: sex was secretive, dirty, humiliating, and painful. There would be other lessons over the years, mostly gleaned from other people's experiences: Sex was for the benefit of men and for having babies. It was something done to women, endured by wives, but not really for their enjoyment. Sexually free women were bad girls. They made great girlfriends, but were not ideal wife material.

Years ago, a college friend who was in a relationship with a guy she really loved shared her concerns along these lines: "I want to marry this man. I am attracted to him, and he wants us to start having sex, but if I do, will I now be labeled a slut? If I sleep with him and he doesn't marry me, then what? But if I don't sleep with him, I think he will leave me. He says he needs me to express my love." She was just shy of her twentieth birthday when she decided to become intimate with him. According to her, the sex was great—so much so that he said she must be a freak. He broke up with her in her final year of college and was engaged to another woman within months. He had shared stories about their sex life with some guys, which negatively affected her reputation. She spiraled into a deep depression. There are too many stories like this, of women trading their bodies for a chance at love. That trade almost always ends in betrayal, heartbreak, and a sullied reputation.

I CAME INTO MY MARRIAGE WITH A LOT OF BAGGAGE THAT I WASN'T EVEN AWARE I HAD.

I came into my marriage with a lot of baggage that I wasn't even aware I had. Focused on building my career, I began to modify my wardrobe to look and feel more corporate. The combination of youth and being a black female in predominantly white academia was not working for me. I couldn't do anything about my age, so instead I subconsciously decided to de-emphasize my femininity so I could be taken more seriously. I was already what many label a D personality. According to the DISC personality assessment system, the D personality style tends to be direct and decisive, and is sometimes described as dominant. They would prefer to lead, not follow, and tend toward leadership and management positions. They tend to have high self-confidence and are risk takers and problem solvers, which enables others to look to them for decisions and direction.

I brought all of that home with me every night. I wanted and needed to be in control. I just assumed I would lead and my husband would follow. I really gave no thought to my husband's needs, and even if I had, I would most likely have dismissed them as his problem and not mine. It never occurred to me that my actions were emasculating to him. This was not his vision for our marriage, so we clashed. I believe that had a detrimental effect on our level of intimacy and our sex life. I spent a lot of time trying to prove to him that I did not need him.

Then came our first child, four miscarriages, and then four more living children. I transitioned from corporate mode to "mother of the year" mode. With so much loss in our lives, it was an easy transition, and one I felt my husband should embrace. By that time, sex was an inconvenience to me. We were happy enough. I was, in my mind, a great wife. Frequent sex was unrealistic. There were always more important tasks to attend to. My wake-up call occurred during a coaching session with one of my clients. When she told her story, it was like looking into a mirror. I thought: How did I get here? Do I like where I am? Do I like how it's impacting the quality of my marriage? What am I willing to do about it?

> **I INTENTIONALLY DISCARDED ANYTHING THAT DID NOT SUPPORT THE MARRIAGE I WANTED AND REPLACED THEM WITH THOUGHTS THAT AFFIRMED ME, MY BODY, AND MY SEXUAL PLEASURE, AS WELL AS MY HUSBAND AND HIS SEXUAL SATISFACTION, AND THAT STRENGTHENED OUR BOND.**

I decided to consciously activate the power of my mind. I did a mental dump of everything I knew and believed about sex and its role in my life. I wrote a mission statement for my marriage and meditated on it daily. I intentionally discarded anything that did not support the marriage I wanted and replaced it with thoughts that affirmed me, my body, and my sexual pleasure, as well as my husband and his sexual satisfaction, and that strengthened our bond. I reclaimed my sexuality. Sex is now not a chore or something to check off my to-do list, it is a pleasure I seek and an expression of the deep and enduring love I have for myself and for my husband.

Today, my "rules" for sex with my husband are as relaxed as they are for meals. You may not always have time for a five-course gourmet meal, but there is always time for a quick bite, a snack on the run, or dessert. Yes, I am still a mother of five and an upstanding member of my community, but none of that precludes me from wanting and enjoying a vibrant sex life with my husband. I took back my sexual power: first in my mind, and then my body responded. What do you desire for you? I encourage you to act now to bring about the changes you want in your marriage in this area.

NOTES

Chapter Eight:
Do You Have the Courage to Be the Best Wife Ever?

We are each other's
harvest:
we are each other's
business:
we are each other's
magnitude and bond.

—Gwendolyn Brooks

The Silent Killer of Relationships

Relationships are destroyed by more than just loud, violent arguments; these tend to be just an obvious symptom of a silent killer. If you are at a crossroads in your marriage, I can guarantee that this silent killer is already at work. Dr. John Gottman identifies in his book *The Seven Principles for Making a Marriage Work* what he calls the Four Horsemen of the Apocalypse: behaviors that, if they occur regularly, are very good predictors of whether your marriage fails or not. Collectively, they are the silent killer of relationships. According to Gottman, the Four Horsemen are:

Criticism versus Complaint

A complaint addresses only the specific action at which your partner has failed. A criticism is global. It attacks the other person's character or personality. Here is an example of a complaint: "I see there is a stain on this shirt; it is one of my favorites." And an example of a criticism: "Must you ruin everything? You get on my last nerve!"

Contempt

Contempt is simply the way we express disgust for a person. While most assume that hate is the opposite of love, I believe indifference and contempt are deadlier than hate. Contempt includes, but is not limited to: sneering, sarcasm, name-calling, eye-rolling, mockery, hostile humor, and condescension. It's primarily transmitted through nonverbal behaviors. Contempt is always disrespectful. Research shows that couples who display contempt for each other suffer more illnesses and diseases than respectful couples do.

Defensiveness

Defensiveness always says, "The problem is not me. It's you." It's a form of deflecting, blaming, and shaming that leaves the other party responsible for any and all conflict. You avoid taking responsibility for your own behavior by pointing to something that someone else did prior to their complaint about you, and thereby refusing to acknowledge that anything is true in what they are saying about your own behavior.

Stonewalling

In relationships where intense arguments break out suddenly, where criticism and contempt lead to defensiveness, and where more contempt leads to more defensiveness, eventually one partner tunes out.

This is the beginning of stonewalling. The stonewaller acts as if he couldn't care less about what the partner is saying or doing. Research indicates that 85 percent of stonewalling in marriages comes from the husbands. Any form of disengagement can be stonewalling.

The Best Wife Ever Pledge

The Four Horsemen corrode the love and respect that is at the core of an intimate relationship. Perhaps you can relate to this in your marriage, and certainly in marriages you have seen. The great news is that there is an antidote to this silent and effective marriage killer. The Best Wife Ever pledge counteracts the Four Horsemen and can eliminate them completely from a marriage.

This pledge was inspired by my oldest son. For months, I watched him intentionally build his relationship with his girlfriend. I was impressed by his thoughtfulness, his attention to the little details, and his consistency. One time, we were out of town on a college visit that included a scholarship interview. Our trip coincided with a major show in which his girlfriend was featured. He wished he could have been there but knew his scholarship opportunity had to take precedence. I found out that, prior to leaving town, he had arranged for his friend to pick up flowers and deliver them to her after the show. Pretty cool, right? Every time I would commend him on how he tended his relationship, he would say, "Mom, I've got this. Don't you know I am the best boyfriend ever?"

One day, after a painful argument with my husband, I was literally thrown for a loop. I was fine with the marriage, but my husband had just indicated he wasn't happy. He loved me. He loved the family we had built. He would never ask for or even want a divorce, but he was hurting. He was hurting because I was seemingly oblivious to his needs. First, I was in denial. Then, I got angry. I wasn't responsible for his happiness. He needed to work that out on his own. You probably already know that anger is simply hurt turned inside out. I was angry at him for asking more of me after all my "sacrifices" for our family.

I was crushed to know my husband was hurting. My ego had taken a beating. How was I so focused on helping and coaching others that I didn't recognize what was going on with him? Feeling defeated, I threw myself a full-blown monster of a pity party. I can still see myself now, crouched in a corner on the cold tile of my bathroom, silently bawling my eyes out. At one point, I stood up to look at myself in the mirror. "Who are you?" I asked. "Whatever happened to the confident, caring, kick-ass young woman who was supposed to have it all? Are you a fraud? How did you make such a mess of your life?" I felt like a failure. Eyes wild and brimming with tears, chest heaving as I gasped for air, I was lost in my misery. I stayed there for longer than I can recall. My husband tried to console me and coax me back to our room, but I was fully committed to my pity party and so I didn't budge. When I was completely cried out, I stood over my sink and stared long and hard at the image in the mirror. I noted my swollen, lifeless eyes and disheveled hair. Tear stains streaked down my cheeks. My shoulders were drooping. I looked like the epitome of hopelessness.

As I stared into my own eyes, the dialogue in my head started to change. "Are you freaking kidding me? So now you are a failure? Where did that stupid thought even spring from? Now you are a victim? Woe is you because things aren't what you think they should be? Where is the woman who fights for her dreams? Where is the power you know lies within? What do you want and what are you willing to do to get it? Lift those shoulders. Dry those tears. Lead your way to a better place so you can lead others there, too. Nothing is easy, nothing changes if you don't put forth the effort. You have work to do. Ain't nobody got time for no pity party!!!"

> MY FOCUS WAS ON ME, DISCARDING THE
> "MEAN GIRL" ROLE I HAD BEEN PLAYING IN MY
> MARRIAGE, SHEDDING THE MEDIOCRITY AND
> COMPLACENCY THAT HAD SEEPED INTO MY
> MARRIAGE, AND STEPPING UP TO INTENTIONALLY
> SOW SEEDS OF LOVE, POSITIVITY, ENCOURAGEMENT,
> APPRECIATION, RESPECT, AND HOPE.

I washed my face with cold water. I straightened up my shoulders and asked myself, "Now what?" Now it was time to rebuild and repair and give the best of myself. I tried to prevaricate at first by insisting that it takes two, that my husband needed to step up as well. But then I thought: Says who? This was not about my husband or even my marriage; it was about myself. It was about committing to being a better version of myself every day. It was about being the best me ever. And as you pursue your best, you will also find that you are the best wife ever. In fact, you can be the best in every role you play if you commit to being your best, and doing it for yourself.

So, I made a pledge to myself that day: for thirty consecutive days, I would commit to doing what I could to be the Best Wife Ever. The focus wasn't on what I hoped my husband's response would be. My focus was on me, discarding the "mean girl" role I had been playing in my marriage, shedding the mediocrity and complacency that had seeped into my marriage, and stepping up to intentionally sow seeds of love, positivity, encouragement, appreciation, respect, and hope. This was about me reconnecting with the best in myself, nurturing those tender areas that had been neglected, knocking down the walls which were ill-serving me, and choosing to live with hope and joy and love, no matter my circumstances.

Initially, I shared the pledge only with one friend, who was also struggling in her marriage. We would check back in with each other and were both amazed at the transformation in our relationships.

Soon, I started challenging a few coaching clients to take the pledge. Within days, they, too had noticed significant changes in how they felt about themselves and their spouses. Instead of constantly harping on their spouses' shortcomings, they changed their focus to the positive aspects of their spouses. When negative thoughts arose, they affirmed their spouses and showed them grace. They went out of their way to do little special things for their husbands. They touched their husbands more. They hugged for no reason. They initiated sex at times and in ways they had never done before. The singular focus was: How do I show up as my best in my marriage today?

> **INSTEAD OF CONSTANTLY HARPING ON THEIR SPOUSES' SHORTCOMINGS, THEY CHANGED THEIR FOCUS TO THE POSITIVE ASPECTS OF THEIR SPOUSES.**

On day eight of her thirty-day pledge, my client Sandy sent me the following email:

I am 52 years old, a grandma, and I'm getting aroused at work just thinking about my husband. What in the world is happening to me? I feel like a sex-crazed teenager. This hasn't happened to me in 30 years. I keep thinking to myself, is this all it takes to make a marriage better? We had a disagreement yesterday, and even that was the gentlest disagreement we have had in years.

Another of my clients, Lynette, had already retained a divorce lawyer and was separated from her husband, the father of her two children, by the time I shared the Best Wife Ever pledge with her. She balked at the pledge because, as she put it, "We are practically divorced already."

"Lynette, what do you have to lose?" I asked. I reminded her that, though it's called the Best Wife Ever pledge, it really is all about her, her focus, and where she chooses to dwell emotionally.

I checked in with Lynette on day nineteen of her pledge. Read our conversation via text below:

LYNETTE: Girl, how about he and I talked for about 30 minutes when we met for him to take the kids.

ME: Really?

LYNETTE: Usually, the sight of him just gets on my last nerve. But today, I complimented him and he complimented me. He said he didn't like how my engine sounded when I pulled up.

ME: Hmmmm . . . .

LYNETTE: He's off tomorrow so he offered to come check the car out for me.

ME: And?

LYNETTE: I said ok. I am looking forward to him stopping by.

ME: Why? You are practically divorced.

LYNETTE: I know. I know. I think I am getting soft.

ME: Soft?

LYNETTE: It's almost like now I know he can't hurt me, I can let my guard down.

ME: He can't hurt you?

LYNETTE: I guess he can, but I still get to choose how I want to feel about things he does. I don't have to be devastated. I have a choice. I can't explain it. I guess I am just more comfortable being the real me with him.

ME: So, what are you saying?

LYNETTE: We cool. I am not sure how it will play out, but the kids are happy we aren't arguing anymore.

ME: So, are you going to stick with the pledge?

LYNETTE: For sure. I like how it makes me feel.

Elisa had finally admitted to herself that she was in an abusive marriage. Her husband had cheated on her at least once. While he never hit her, there were times she suspected he was on the verge of doing so. Twelve years of his verbal and emotional abuse had taken a toll on her psyche. Pressure from her relatives to stay in her marriage and not bring shame to her family wasn't helping either. She had recently been diagnosed with hypertension. She was stressed out and in a depressed state when her sister brought her to one of my women's seminars. Elisa was willing to take the thirty-day pledge just to buy some peace in her home while she figured things out. A week after she began the pledge, I received a call from her. She said she had some good news and just had to share it with me: "The pledge is changing my life. I was so angry and hurt and beaten down that I couldn't see any light or anything good in my life. I don't know if my husband has even noticed that I am putting in a lot of effort to be loving and considerate toward him, but it doesn't even matter, because I am finally being loving to myself. Yesterday, as I was getting dressed, I complimented myself. I have never complimented myself. Usually, when I see my image, I hear my husband's negative comments. It felt good. I started laughing out loud. I like this pledge."

Can you feel it? A movement has begun. The Best Wife Ever pledge is transformative. It first transforms you and then it positively impacts how you see and interact with your spouse. I am excited for the women who are already part of this movement, and I am looking forward to hearing how this pledge changes your life as well.

For those who want to take this even further, I recommend you commit to the Best Wife Ever sixty-six-day pledge. Although many experts still teach that it takes 21–30 days for a new activity to become habit, new research indicates the range is actually 18–254 days, with the average being sixty-six days. Since I don't live for minimums, I decided to go beyond the thirty-day pledge and commit to a sixty-six-day pledge. Essentially, my goal is to make this pledge a lifestyle. If you can live the pledge for sixty-six days, being your best will become part of how you are wired to see and engage with the world.

Change Is from the Inside Out

The Bible states that we speak out of the abundance of our hearts. To put it a different way, our words are always a reflection of the internal dialogue in our heads. The beauty of the Best Wife Ever pledge is that it encourages a change on the inside. It would be very difficult to consistently express love to someone without, as a result, retraining your mind to think loving thoughts.

A popular folktale illustrates the power of retraining your mind and changing your perspective for the better. A grandmother was concerned about how her granddaughter was responding to having been a victim of bullying. She felt the teen was allowing the incident to change her personality for the worse. She invited her granddaughter into the kitchen to assist with some preparations.

On the counter, she laid out an egg, a teabag, and some carrots. She asked her granddaughter to examine all three items and then to put water in three separate pots and heat them on the stovetop. Into one pot, the grandmother placed the egg. Into the second pot, she placed the carrots. Into the third and final pot, she placed the teabag. After twenty minutes, she asked the granddaughter to take all three pots off the stove and share her observations on the contents of each pot.

The granddaughter grudgingly went along with her grandmother. Of the carrot, she said, "Ewwww…it's all mushy and stuff. I like my carrots firm and crunchy." As she picked up the egg, her grandmother asked her to crack it. She cracked the egg and successfully peeled off its shell. She noted that the egg was firm to the touch. Finally, she got to the teabag. She reported, "Not much going on here, Grandma. The teabag is wet but not much else changed."

Her grandma said, "Take a closer look."

The granddaughter asked, "Grandma, what is this all about?"

Her grandma responded, "I thought you would never ask. Each of these items was subjected to the same condition—boiling water. The carrots started out firm but ended mushy. The egg started as a liquid but became firm. The teabag appears to have remained the same, but it is the only item that also changed the water in which it was boiled. The bullying you have experienced must have felt like being immersed in hot water. Which of these items best represents how you think you have responded to the incident?"

"I didn't go mushy so I am not the carrot. I don't know what to make of the teabag, so I probably would be most like the egg. I got hard because I needed to protect myself."

"You are right; I have observed that you did go hard. These last few weeks you've been mean-spirited, even around here. Observe the teabag. Of all the items, this is the only one that changed the water instead of just letting the water change it. It allowed the hot water to bring out its essence and flavors, and instead of being changed, it brought about change. You could be like the teabag if you so choose. When you are faced with adversity, don't let it change you by making you too soft or hard, instead let it bring out the best of what is on the inside of you. Use the adversity to bring about change in your environment and leave your environment better than you found it. In life, there will always be challenges. The question is, how do you show up and meet those challenges? Concentrate on building yourself on the inside. That way, when you are pressed or stressed, only good flows from you."

> IN LIFE, THERE WILL ALWAYS BE CHALLENGES. THE QUESTION IS, HOW DO YOU SHOW UP AND MEET THOSE CHALLENGES?

The grandmother's advice applies to all of us, especially as you embark on the Best Wife Ever pledge. It is not easy to change old habits. Depending on both what has transpired to get you to this point in your marriage and the personality of your spouse, consistently showing love for thirty straight days may make you feel like you've been thrown into a cauldron of boiling water. To set yourself up for success in this process, and to help you deal with the hurts you may face, you should have a plan to build yourself up. I strongly recommend using affirmations while focusing on your life purpose statement as a guiding force for all your choices. When you fill yourself with light, no matter what pressures this challenge or your circumstances present, only love and light will flow from you. Below are a few affirmations to get you started.

Sample Affirmations

- I am love; I give love and I receive love.

- The power that created the universe resides in me. Everything is lining up for my own good.

- Every circumstance makes me a better version of myself. I love everything about me.

- I give and receive the support I need to achieve my highest dreams.

- Life supports me fully.

- I give and receive respect.

- I now let go of negative thinking and negative experiences.

- The impossible is possible for me.

- The four winds of success are blowing into my life. I love myself.

- I am smart, strong, and capable of achieving my life purpose. I live with joy.

- Endless good comes to me in endless ways.

- I am beautiful.

- I am at peace in my own body.

- I release all my limiting beliefs about myself.

- I transmit harmony to everyone I encounter.

- I am whole and complete. I am irresistible.

- Divine order is at work in my mind, body, and affairs. My husband and children rise up and call me blessed. My husband is satisfied in my arms.

- I give thanks for my whirlwind success. I am harmonious, poised, and magnetic.

- It is easy for me to assert myself with love.

- I move easily with the flow of life. I am a magnet for love.

- I choose to experience kindness and compassion.

- I am thankful for my life.

- I love with my whole heart.

- I easily forgive myself and all others.

- Peace dwells in and emanates from me.

- I cheerfully embrace my present and future. I let go of all that hinders me.

- I accept my whole self: mind, body, and spirit.

- I nourish my body, mind, and soul.

- My greatest expectations come to pass in miraculous ways.

- Everything I need is within me now.

- I easily tap into the best of me.

- I love my life.

- I choose faith.

- I take responsibility for my actions and words.

- I have the courage to make tough decisions.

- I celebrate me!

- I am willing to feel delicate, painful emotions in order to set them free.

- I choose to remain present with both the good and the not-so-good in my life.

- I accept pain as an inevitable part of life.

- I take charge of my finances in a responsible and accurate way.

- I choose foods now that will support the body I desire to have in the future.

- I focus on things that are in my control.

* * *

This is a game changer, I guarantee it. No matter where you are in your marriage today, if you accept and execute this pledge for thirty consecutive days, you will transform your relationship with yourself and with your spouse. It will either be the springboard for you to go on and build a mutually fulfilling marriage or serve as the foundation for a respectful and even loving breakup. Whatever you eventually choose to do about your marriage, this pledge will make it easier to navigate.

When you embrace the entirety of this pledge, you are guaranteeing a better understanding of yourself, a deeper connection to your core, and a more meaningful life. I can hardly wait to hear your great news.

For ongoing support with your Best Wife Ever pledge, join the Reclaim Your Life community at www.wivesatthecrossroads.com/bestwifeeverpledge.

NOTES

Chapter Nine:
Overcoming Life's Hurdles

Remember, life is for living and learning.
So listen to your life and the lessons it offers.

—Susan L. Taylor

Congratulations! You've covered a lot of ground and made it this far. That is admirable because a high percentage of people who purchase books like this never open them, and even fewer read all the way through. It's like the exercise equipment and DVDs that end up prominently featured at our garage sales. We meant well when we purchased them. We fully intended to use the product as described. We had a problem the product was designed to solve, we were even convinced it was the key to solving our problem, but somehow, we still never got around to putting it to use—at least, not long enough to reap any benefits.

So, let's start at the very beginning. Of the over one million books published annually in the US alone, and of all the options you have to spend your money on, you chose to invest in this book. Why is that? I am going to guess that something about the author, the title, or a recommendation you received from another resonated with a challenge you may be currently experiencing. I was very specific with my title because I wrote this book for very special women who mean a lot to me.

I wrote this book for the beautiful woman who has given the best she knows how to give but is stunned and confused that she nevertheless may be looking at a failing marriage. I wrote this book for the woman who feels she has exhausted her options and still cannot get the man she loves to love, support, and cherish her as she desires. I wrote this book for the woman who had high hopes and beautiful dreams for her family and the life she would build with her husband, who is now crushed as she watches that dream slowly but surely disintegrate and float off in the winds of uncertainty. I wrote this book for my fellow sisters who never thought it possible that they would become a part of the infamous divorce statistic. I wrote this book for me, because, when I noticed the cracks in the foundation of my marriage, I was determined to address the fault lines within myself. I had to eliminate the frustration and fear within so I could move forward in love. I know that when we operate in love, the outcome must be love. I wrote this book for you, and I thank you for reading it.

> **I WROTE THIS BOOK FOR THE WOMAN WHO FEELS SHE HAS EXHAUSTED HER OPTIONS AND STILL CANNOT GET THE MAN SHE LOVES TO LOVE, SUPPORT, AND CHERISH HER LIKE SHE DESIRES.**

However, we must go beyond just acquiring knowledge. Contrary to popular belief, it is the application of knowledge, and not just the mere possession of it, that brings about power. If all you do is read this book and take no action, I will have fallen short of my goal for you: to join the movement to reclaim your life and build a new life that honors and fulfills you.

Why would a person read this book and yet not apply the strategies within, even when their marriage is falling apart and they have no other solutions? Force of habit? I recently met a widow with three school-aged children. Her husband owned an insurance agency, but when he passed away suddenly and prematurely, to her utter dismay and frustration she found out that he had never purchased a life insurance policy for himself. He sold insurance to others, he clearly understood the value of life insurance, but obviously he kept putting off purchasing his own. Today, his widow struggles to provide for their family. He was a good man, but like many good and smart people, we don't always do what we know we should.

Wanting to bring about change in your marriage and personal life and actually achieving success in these areas are two totally different things. There are many reasons why we don't follow through on things that we should. Can you think of some reasons you've sabotaged your own success in the past? To improve your chances of success in living the life you desire, it is helpful to examine potential obstacles to your success, so you can anticipate and plan to minimize them. Some likely deterrents include:

Distractions or Lack of Focus

We are bombarded with information and a plethora of distractions at any given time. In the palm of my hand, I have access to the World Wide Web, thousands of social media followers, emails, and so much more. It should come as no surprise that over 90 percent of my clients identified lack of focus as their biggest obstacle to success. Do you tend to jump from one great idea to another? Do you have multiple projects you've started but not completed? When we lack focus, we limit our results and eventually convince ourselves to quit in favor of the next best thing. Distractions are a form of procrastination.

Did you complete all the assignments in the earlier chapters of this book, or did you start and then convince yourself that you would finish the book and then go back to complete the exercises? Be honest.

Fear

Many people never get started because they are overcome by fear. To address a fear, you must first identify the fear. In the past, when you have been paralyzed by fear, what were you afraid of? Some have a fear of success. Others live lives of mediocrity because they are afraid of aiming higher and possibly failing. Sometimes, fear is born out of a sense of worthlessness. People limit themselves for fear of rejection. What fear do you currently face that may prevent you from applying the lessons in this book? How will you overcome this fear as you move forward?

Lack of Money

How many times have you turned your back on an opportunity that could change your life because you were convinced you could not afford it? As you move forward, you may discover that it will be helpful for you to work with a counselor, a coach, or an attorney, or to seek out additional professional assistance. You may immediately dismiss that recommendation based on your resources, even when it is to your detriment not to get the help. Such decisions can derail your success. As Henry Ford famously said, "If you think you can't, you are right. If you think you can, you are also right." Ultimately, you must deem yourself worthy of the investment to create and live your dreams.

Time

The perceived lack of time is one of the top excuses people give for their lack of follow through. How often have you convinced yourself that the reason you did not honor a prior commitment was because you had no time? For the most part, we do make time for what we really want to do. I have worked with women who are convinced they have no time to exercise even as they share the latest on their favorite TV show. As you think about the assignments in this book, from your life purpose statement to planning out a road map for your goals to implementing the thirty-day pledge, what is your plan to make time to follow through?

Conflict

When conflicts arise—and they almost always do—we tend to get confused. What now? Faced with this additional obstacle, many abandon their original plan, become frozen by indecision, or fall back into old, unhealthy habits.

Poor Attitude

Your attitude toward your life and your marriage will be a main determinant of your outcome. If you are skeptical, close-minded, or negative about the prospects of a positive outcome, that will limit your success.

Self-Doubt

The challenges you are experiencing in your marriage have undoubtedly taken a toll on you. This could cause an increase in self-doubt. Lack of confidence disguised as self-doubt is a major barrier that prevents people from achieving their goals.

Listening to the Doubters and Naysayers

Misery loves company, and the company you keep will affect the choices you make. As you attempt to employ the lessons in this book, be mindful to avoid listening to negative comments and messages from family, friends, or acquaintances. Negativity kills progress every time.

Laziness

We are creatures of habit. It's very tempting and easy to slip back into old, lazy habits. The changes you desire in your life will not just happen on their own; you will have to work intelligently and consistently to see the results you desire.

> ### IT IS NOT NECESSARILY THE MOST TALENTED WHO RISE TO THE TOP OR LIVE LIFE ON THEIR OWN TERMS; SUCCESS FAVORS THOSE WHO CAN MAKE BOLD DECISIONS AND ACT ON THEM REGARDLESS OF THE OBSTACLES.

The Courage to Act

Your destiny is determined by the timing and quality of your decisions. It is not necessarily the most talented who rise to the top or live life on their own terms; success favors those who can make bold decisions and act on them regardless of the obstacles. In coaching and working with women over the past few decades, there are generally three kinds of people that I have observed: those who make things happen; those who watch things happen; and those who wonder what happened. I call them the CEOs, the Stargazers, and the Victims.

CEOs

This group is made up of the ones that make things happen. They assess their situation, they take full responsibility for their lives, and they make decisions and act decisively. Things may not always work out exactly as they planned, but they choose to be fully present in determining the direction and outcome of their lives. They are always willing to make any necessary adjustments to accomplish their goals.

They tend to exhibit more self-confidence and live more fulfilling lives. Women in this category are more likely to use phrases that begin with "I will . . ." or "I have . . . ."

Stargazers

This group consists of the dreamers; they watch things happen. Intrinsically, they know they should do something about their circumstances, but their default setting is to hope and pray that things work out on their own without ever having to get uncomfortable themselves. Someone once said to me, "Hope is not a plan." We definitely should live hopeful, faith-filled lives, but even the Bible reminds us that faith without works is dead. This group is more likely to use phrases such as "I hope . . ." or "I wish . . . ."

Victims

This group is where the non-decision-makers tend to gather. They wonder what in the world happened and why it is happening to them. They see themselves as helpless to change their situations and, as a coping mechanism, to ignore issues until things implode.

They live their lives reacting to one hardship after another. They rarely ever get ahead of their problems or position themselves for success because they are convinced they have no power to create their lives, so they don't even try. Phrases most likely to be heard from members of this group are "I can't . . ." and "I didn't . . . ."

You have a decision to make. You can be a stargazer, choose to take no action on what you have read, and just hope and pray things work out in your life and marriage. You can play the victim and never experience the richness of your talents and purpose. Or you can choose to be the CEO—the chief executive officer of your life. You can recognize that the buck stops with you. You can engage your power to make your dreams into your reality. You can be the one who will complete the assignments in this book and create an action plan for your long-term success. You can embrace resources to help you turn your current situation around—and I will be cheering for you all the way.

I have some questions for you. What is your current situation costing you? Where do you feel the pain? Are you carrying your stress in your gut and experiencing intestinal issues? Do you feel it in your forehead, at the back of back of your neck, or in your lower back? What coping mechanisms have you employed? Are you eating more? Not eating enough? Are you drinking a glass of wine or something stronger to take the edge off? Are you planning multiple events to "escape" your life? Are you praying all the time? Have you thrown yourself into work or your children because that's your safe haven? Are you having emotional or physical liaisons that are unhealthy for you? Are you constantly worrying about your security? Are you distracted from growing your career? Are you sad and disengaged? How much will a contested or acrimonious divorce cost you—monetarily and emotionally? What are the long-term costs if you don't actively pursue the right solution to your dilemma, now?

Moving from Frustration to Peace

Do you remember Lynette's story? She's my coaching client who, by the time we met, had already retained a divorce attorney. She had reluctantly agreed to take the thirty-day Best Wife Ever pledge. Although she was skeptical—and had the additional challenge that she and her husband were already living apart—she still committed to daily expressing love to him. She said it was super awkward, as she did not want him to think she was pursuing him. She set up a coaching session with me, and together we identified her desired outcomes for the pledge.

Lynette had been hurt by her husband's infidelity and felt he had never seen her as an equal or cared about meeting her emotional needs. She had been very lonely in her marriage; she reached a point where she could no longer stomach his disrespect and lack of emotional or moral support. Although she was concerned about the potential impact of a divorce on their two boys, she had reached the end of her rope. Her husband refused to go to counseling. Her hope was that, through the Best Wife Ever pledge, she could heal from his betrayal, forgive herself for ignoring the warning signs before she married him, and grow personally so she could make better choices in the future. She wanted them to reach a place of mutual understanding and respect so they could effectively co-parent their sons and minimize the negative effects of the divorce on the kids.

Lynette was acting like the CEO of her life; by the time she completed the thirty-day pledge, she said she had never felt more connected to her husband. He wanted them to try again. She did, too, but she didn't trust that it was anything but a temporary emotional decision for him and she worried he would hurt her again. She sought the advice of her girlfriends. Some pointed out how hard it was to find a man and encouraged her to take him back. Others reminded her of the affairs, the tears, even the time she had to call a friend to bring her and her newborn baby back from the hospital because she could not reach her husband. She was confused. In her confusion, Lynette morphed into a stargazer. She would leave all the decisions in her husband's hands and just hope and believe that what was meant to be, would be.

Her husband moved back in with Lynette and their boys. Things were good for a while, but one Friday he didn't come home. Her heart sank. She had been here before. He finally called her on Saturday evening. He said he just needed time to clear his head. He explained, "It's not you; it's me." She reached out to me. Her first words were, "I can't believe this is happening to me again." Lynette had just adopted a victim's mentality.

A significant part of your success and your ability to move your life in the direction in which you want to go will hinge on surrounding yourself with the right input and support. Watch any great athlete who enjoys long-term success and you will note that they have a team. Serena Williams, the most outstanding athlete of her time, has a team. Behind the scenes she has created a support system, one that includes a tennis coach, a hitting partner, a nutritionist, a physical therapist, and a personal assistant. She even hires life coaches to help her with the mental aspect of her life and game.

> **A SIGNIFICANT PART OF YOUR SUCCESS AND YOUR ABILITY TO MOVE YOUR LIFE IN THE DIRECTION IN WHICH YOU WANT TO GO WILL HINGE ON SURROUNDING YOURSELF WITH THE RIGHT INPUT AND SUPPORT.**

What derailed Lynette? She was already on the path from frustration to peace in her life, so what happened? She lost sight of the goals she had set. She listened to people ill-equipped to help her get where she wanted to go. She gave up her power. She allowed herself to be led by fear, not love. What choices will you make?

You met Elisa in the last chapter. She had invested twelve years into a marriage in which her husband verbally and emotionally abused her. Elisa loved her husband and still believed that it was God's will for them to remain married, but things only got worse. Her children could see how he treated her and she knew she was not in a healthy place.

Elisa decided to work with me as her life coach. She was singularly focused on empowering herself so she could have better financial options if she decided to leave her marriage. Elisa continued the Best Wife Ever pledge and also added on other tools I recommended to her. She committed to a daily regimen designed to bring about a mindset shift for herself. She had to first overcome the negative programming of her childhood as well as override the negative voice of her husband in her head. Amongst other strategies, we used "accelerated learning" techniques, including the power of declarations.

How does this work? She created a series of affirmations reflecting herself as her ideal self rather than her current state. Multiple times a day, she would first put her hand on her heart and make a verbal declaration, then touch her head with her index finger and make another verbal declaration. What is a declaration? It is an affirmative statement that you speak out loud with emphasis and energy.

Elisa took her focus off her husband and his issues. She focused on growing the light within herself. The shift from using affirmations to declarations is powerful on a number of levels. The energy you put into your declaration carries its own vibrational frequency. When you speak your affirmation loudly and with great energy, that energy vibrates through the cells of your body; and when you touch your heart and head as you are saying it, your words resonate at a deeper level, sending powerful messages to your subconscious mind.

As we worked together, Elisa's mother needed assistance after a surgery and temporarily moved in with Elisa's family. She received an unexpected promotion at work. It was more pay, but also included some travel, which put a strain on her family since her husband didn't believe he had to help maintain the household. Eight months into our coaching, Elisa talked and walked like a different woman. Her husband didn't berate her so much anymore, probably because he was not getting the reaction he wanted. She had been diligently rebuilding her credit and saving money for her own place when she was advised to have a hysterectomy. She informed her husband, and the surgery was scheduled.

On the day of her surgery, her husband told her that, instead of staying to support her, he was leaving for a three-day conference. Elisa called me before she was taken to the pre-op room. She told me, "I am filing for divorce. I have an appointment with my attorney next week."

"Are you certain this is what you want?" I asked.

"Yes, I am ready. I have applied the principles you've taught me, I have done all I can do in this marriage, and I am ready for the next chapter of my life. I deserve better. My sons deserve better. The world deserves my best, and despite my best efforts, I have determined that my marriage is too toxic an environment for me to thrive."

Elisa's divorce has been finalized. She has no regrets. She knows she gave it her best. On the day the divorce was finalized, she wrote her now ex-husband a love letter expressing her gratitude for both the good parts of their marriage and the lessons she learned from the challenging times. She says, "I will marry again, at the right time, to the right one, for the right reasons, and the right way, because I will do it all from love and not fear." Elisa is now training to be a life coach.

NOTES

CHAPTER TEN:
WINNERS TAKE ACTION

You have to have confidence in your ability,
and then be tough enough to follow through.

—Rosalynn Carter

So, what now? What should you do? Where do you start? How do you get from where you are to where you want to be? Are you feeling even more overwhelmed at your situation and the choices open to you?

I hope you have enjoyed reading this book and that you have gained some great insights, but more importantly, I hope you use the six steps I have outlined to dramatically transform your life. If you believe, as I do, that the only limits we experience are the ones we place on ourselves, when is a better time than now for you to raise your limits? When is a better time to seize your power to choose where you dwell each day?

My dream for you is that you've awakened every cell in your body, shifting your mindset and sending a singular message to every cell that says, "I am peace, I am love, and I live the life I desire." My hope for you is that you choose to join the movement of women loving life, living fully, and spreading love.

But, as much as I want the best for you, no one but yourself can change your condition. Why? Because you alone can choose what thoughts you focus on and let take root in your life. The women reading this book and hoping for change are just as likely to be living in million-dollar homes as they are to be living paycheck to paycheck. We often look to externals to explain our frustrations, but the truth is far simpler.

> **MY DREAM FOR YOU IS THAT YOU'VE AWAKENED EVERY CELL IN YOUR BODY, SHIFTING YOUR MINDSET AND SENDING A SINGULAR MESSAGE TO EVERY CELL THAT SAYS, "I AM PEACE, I AM LOVE, AND I LIVE THE LIFE I DESIRE."**

Your thoughts determine the quality of your life. Your thoughts will determine where you dwell and how you live. If you are willing to do the mental and internal work to transform your thoughts, you can create the life you desire. There is no progress and no achievement without the sacrifice to develop your plans and their implementation. Your level of sacrifice will determine your results. Reading this book is a start, but if you want to see real change in your life, it will be your actions that will make the difference.

Let's review where we've been so far on this journey together. In chapter one, I shared my story. I can write and coach about transforming your life and marriage because I have successfully done this in mine. I introduced a truth you must embrace to move forward: that the results you see in your life are always about you and how you show up in your life. There has always been oppression in the world, but what really determines people's lives is how they respond to their circumstances rather than the circumstances themselves. You must embrace this truth, otherwise you will always be tempted to believe you are powerless to improve your life.

In chapter two, we established that the challenges you are facing in your marriage are unfortunately neither new nor unique to you. Whatever is putting pressure on your marriage has befallen others, and they survived it. Some survived with their marriages strengthened while some left their marriages to get the healing they needed to powerfully live the rest of their lives. In chapter three, I gave you an overview of the six steps available to you to move yourself from a place of frustration to a place of peace. If you completed the assignments in chapter four, you not only have a life purpose statement that will serve as a compass, letting you know what direction to take in life, you also took an inventory of your life using the Eneli Abundant Life Scale. This will have both given you clarity about where you stand in the most important areas of your life and helped you identify what you really want for your life. It should have been a very exhilarating and empowering exercise for you because most of us do not grow up hearing that we have real choices, as usually the choices are being made for us. Having choices can be scary, especially for those who have had limited practice in making their own.

Beware of the voices in your head convincing you that you do not actually have to complete the exercises. That will make this book about as effective as lying down and watching a bunch of fitness trainers exercise would be. You may have been temporarily entertained, perhaps even inspired, but you will experience no transformation; and, if anything, you will further condition your mind to believe you are powerless to change your life. Get out of your comfort zone. Overcome that tendency to procrastinate or to be lazy. Go back and get it done.

Chapters five, six, and seven were all about you. Who are you? Really, who are you? What are your strengths? How can you use your strengths to fulfill your life purpose? How do you mitigate your weaknesses? In these chapters, I reaffirmed your power and obligation to LEAD yourself through self-love, education, action, and the willingness to distinguish yourself. And then we explored what is still taboo for so many women: your right to sex and intimacy on your terms. Chapter eight is my favorite because there I affirm that the purity of love is absolute. If you can learn to express love freely, rather than out of fear (which negates love) or obligation, that love you give transforms you and comes back to you in a way that defies description. It's like asking the sleep-deprived mother of a newborn to express why she loves her baby so much. Though the baby can't even smile at her yet, let alone express gratitude, the purity of her love for her child fills all voids. Finally, in chapter nine, we reviewed the obstacles you will undoubtedly face as you apply the lessons from this book.

So what now? I strongly recommend that you read through this book again, this time making sure you do all the exercises. Commit to reviewing this book once a month for the next year. Why? Because repetition is the mother of learning. As you apply the lessons in your life, you will have questions and face doubts. Re-reading this book will help you stay the course even when you are tempted to quit, and I guarantee you will be tempted to quit. The more you review the information in this book and go over your own responses, the greater your clarity and ability to change your life. In addition, though many think they can snap their fingers and change everything in their lives, it is worthwhile to recognize that new habits take time. Be gentle with yourself even as you push toward your goals.

As you continue this journey, you may be inclined to seek out the advice of family or friends versus advice from a professional. I totally understand that. But remember, we are trying to shift your mindset to help you create the life of your dreams. It would be foolhardy, when building a home, to only take advice from someone who has never built one instead of looking to someone with more knowledge or experience. Successful people seek advice from those who are more accomplished than they are. I always say, "Don't seek advice from anyone with whom you wouldn't want to switch places." The only exception is if they are sharing what not to do. Instead, I highly recommend you consider hiring a personal life coach that's a good fit for you. A good coach will help you accelerate and maintain your successes.

Why Coaching?

There are many reasons why you might find it helpful to work with a coach to achieve your desired goals. Some of these are:

Focus

Coaches help you identify and focus your energy on what will make the biggest difference for you. They help you get clarity on what really matters.

Structure

Coaches provide a structure that cuts through time wasters and distractions. They teach you proven success tools and strategies to eliminate unnecessary frustration.

Accountability and Support

Willpower fades. Good intentions wilt. A coach will hold you accountable to what you say you want for your life. They will support you when you are tempted to quit and help you identify strategies to keep moving forward.

Help with Blind Spots

Coaches help you figure out what you don't know and they clue you in to things you may not be able to see. They will be honest with you because they are not vested in any specific outcome.

Competitive Advantage

A coach can help you get from one point to another faster than you could on your own.

Leadership Skills

Coaches model leadership, which you can emulate, by employing powerful questioning techniques. Using these can help you become a better listener and a more effective person.

Motivation

Sometimes you just don't have the motivation on your own to stay focused consistently enough to accomplish your goals. I wrote this book with the help of a writing coach because I needed that extra motivation.

Wisdom

Having someone committed to your goals, who condenses your learning curve and gives you feedback as things change, is priceless.

Peace of Mind

Because coaches help you identify and align your values and clear guilt-trips and pity parties, they help you increase your personal and professional fulfillment.

As I stated earlier, I have had to learn and apply these lessons in my own life to create the life and marriage I want. Now it is my turn to teach others. As I do so, I strive to empower, inspire, equip, and support women to live their dreams and not their frustrations.

I leave you with these words:

You are amazing.
You are unique.
You are a gift like no other.
The pain you've borne,
The scars you wear,
Are proof of your power.
You are resilient.
You are smart.
Don't you dare cower.
The world awaits
Your dreams' great fate;
For you were born to inspire.

I wish you love, peace, and much success.
Here's to Reclaiming Your Life,

Aya

Website:	www.WivesAtTheCrossroads.com
Blog:	www.ayaeneli.com/blog
	linkedin.com/ayafubaraeneli
f	facebook.com/wivesatthecrossroads
🐦	@AyaEneli
📷	aya_eneli

NOTES

A Personal Invitation

Congratulations! You finished the book and that puts you in rare company because many people buy books they never read or complete.

So, what decisions have you made as a result of reading this book? The tools and strategies I have shared in this book will work for you, but only if you don't actively apply them. The results in your life are dependent on your actions.

Throughout this book we talked about taking the personal responsibility to reclaim your life, the life you dream about. Acting now can transform all areas of your life – your relationships, finances, health, career, personal growth, happiness and overall success, and just as importantly, reclaiming your life sets you up to help others reclaim theirs too.

As you figured out with your life purpose statement, reclaiming life is not just about you, it is about making a positive impact on the world around you.

We encourage you to join us online to help you stay on track with your daily habits and your pledge. This will be a forum where you can be a part of a positive group of like-minded women—a place where we can grow and support the transformation of women across the globe.

I look forward to connecting with you there!

Aya

ADDITIONAL RESOURCES

We have a wide array of products and services designed to support individuals and organizations who serve women.

Be sure to visit www.wivesatthecrossroads.com and click on "FREE BOOK BONUSES" to receive additional resources that include:

- The Monthly Marriage Checkup List
- A printable list of declarations
- The Best Wife Ever "thought of the week"

From my heart to yours, I invite you to attend the three-day Reclaim Your Life Retreat. This retreat will take you to a higher level of success in every area of your life. You will confront your limiting beliefs and create new paradigms and mindset for your life.

In one weekend, you will discover parts of yourself you had forgotten and will leave renewed with a brand-new mindset for success in every area of your life. This retreat is so powerful and essential to your success that for a limited time, we have decided to provide a two for one ticket option for readers of this book. That's right, your spouse or a friend come *free!* For more details about this offer, visit www.wivesatthecrossroads.com/retreat.

You can buy a copy of my book, *Live Your Abundant Life*, on Amazon, but I'm happy to stick a complimentary copy in the mail to you—autographed, and with a few other secret treats and surprises, too. Here's what you have to do to get it:

1. Schedule a Strategy Session with my team at www.wivesatthecrossroads/Apply

2. Show up to the Strategy Session—No shows and cancelations will not be rewarded.

3. On your call, let us know you'd like us to send you a free copy of the book.

When you get the book (and all the other surprises in the Reclaim Your Power care package), be sure to drop a review on Amazon or post a picture of yourself holding the book on Facebook or Instagram! *This complimentary book offer is open to the first hundred people who meet the requirement.*

HAVE AYA FUBARA ENELI
SPEAK AT YOUR EVENT!

AYA WILL INSPIRE ATTENDEES AT YOUR EVENT TO GET MORE CLARITY ABOUT WHAT THEY WANT OUT OF LIFE AND TAKE ACTION TO CREATE THE LIFE THEY DESIRE.

Most conference and event planners spend considerable time, effort, and money providing new information and strategies to their audience, and yet there almost always remains a big gap between learning new concepts and applying them.

"KNOWLEDGE ISN'T POWER;

APPLIED KNOWLEDGE IS POWER!"

Maybe it's time to give them what they really need – understanding of why they don't execute and a system to help them execute. Great information is not enough. Growth and transformation only occurs when information is applied. Let Aya teach your audience what it takes to implement at a high level and achieve their goals and desires using simple 5-step system.

Aya's engaging and interactive sessions range from a one-hour keynote to a one-day workshop, and offer fresh insight into what it takes to achieve greatness.

TO HIRE AYA TO SPEAK AT YOUR EVENT:

Visit: www.ayaeneli.com
Call us at: (512) 956-6025
Email us at info@ayaeneli.com

RECLAIM YOUR
LIFE COACH

For many people, the greatest barrier to achieving their dreams isn't desire or even know-how; the most common challenge is overcoming old habits and limiting beliefs.

To assist you in applying the concepts covered in this book, we offer coaching support. Studies have shown that coaching can improve your outcomes by up to 95 percent.

For more information on our coaching program,
visit www.wivesatthecrossroads.com/coaching.

REFERENCES

Gottman, John. (1994). Why Marriages Succeed or Fail. New York NY: Simon & Schuster.

Eggerichs, E. (2004). Love & Respect. Nashville TN: Thomas Nelson.

Ethridge, S. (2008). The Sexually Confident Wife: Connecting with Your Husband Mind Body Heart Spirit. New York NY: Crown Archetypes.

Cutrer, W., Glahn S. (2007). Sexual Intimacy in Marriage. Grand Rapids MI: Kregel Publications.

Omartian, S. (1997). The Power of a Praying Wife. Eugene OR: Harvest House Publishers.

Wagner, C.P. (2005). Discover Your Spiritual Gifts. Ventura CA: Regal Books.

Chapman, G.(1995) The Five Love Languages: How to Express Heartfelt Commitment to Your Mate. Chicago IL: Northfield Publishing.

Wilcox, B. (2011) Why Marriage Matters: Thirty Conclusions from the Social Sciences (3rd ed.). Chicago, IL: Broadway Publications;

Fubara Eneli, A. (2004) Live Your Abundant Life: Encouragement and Strategies to Create a Meaningful and Fulfilled Life. Maitland, FL: Xulon Press.

California Healthy Marriages Coalition. (2008) Healthy Marriages, Healthy Lives: Research on the Alignment of Health, Marital Outcomes and Marriage Education (This is a booklet by a corporate author in Fairfax, VA).

Testimony of Dr. Barbara Dafoe Whitehead, National Marriage Project, before the US Senate Subcommittee on Children and Families.

Harrar, Sari., DeMaria, Rita. (2007) The 7 Stages of Marriage: Laughter, Intimacy and Passion Today. Pleasantville, NY : Reader's Digest Association.

Leider, Richard. (1997) The Power of Purpose: Creating Meaning in Your Life and Work. Oakland, CA: Brett-Koehler Publications.

Tugavela, Vironika. (2013) The Love Mindset. England: Soulux Press

ACKNOWLEDGMENTS

I am eternally grateful to the "village" that has helped make me who I am today. I have been fortunate to have been loved and nurtured by some amazing people across countries, continents, and oceans. To my earliest teachers and mentors, I thank you for all you invested in me and for teaching me to believe in myself.

There are a few women who in their own ways challenged me to strive to be my best, to live with love and dignity, to serve others with humility, to own my power, and to never settle for a relationship that does not affirm the best of who I am:

Mrs. Ngozi Iyizoba Okongwu inspired me to always aim for excellence and to have the courage to be me. Aunty Malikah Faquir epitomized love and was fearless in her pursuit of a loving relationship. She taught me to accept and nurture all of me and to be proud of my heritage. Elsie Blount probably wasn't even aware of what an impact she had on me, but I watched her speak truth to power, love her husband, and raise amazing daughters. Dr. Marianne Williams loved me like her own, welcoming me into her home and teaching me how to balance my youthful fervor with wisdom. Lee Smith, who I affectionately call Mama Lee, saw beyond my exterior into my soul and nurtured me in an environment that would have otherwise consumed me. Ruth Sallee Gresham gave of her heart and wisdom and showed me how to handle difficult situations with grace and strength. The phenomenal Dr. Valerie Lee proved to me that I could indeed have it all—a thriving career, an intimate relationship with God, a loving and supportive husband, and well-adjusted, successful children. Each of these women came into my life during my formative years, and each planted and watered seeds in me which have greatly shaped who I am today.

Special thanks to my clients over the years who have trusted me with their hopes and dreams, and whose challenges and triumphs have helped me create this body of work. Thanks to all who've read my social media posts and columns through the years and have encouraged me to serve even more people. Annie Dockery, thanks for the gift of your photography. Natalie Creasy, you came through for me in a big way. Angela Lauria, you expanded my scope of what I thought possible. Thank you. Kristen Carmona, thank you for supporting my vision to impact women worldwide.

I am grateful to my children, who've challenged me to live what I preach. You all are my greatest motivators. I give glory to my heavenly Father who continues to guide my path and teach me lessons from both the high and the low points of my life.

Finally, my deepest gratitude goes to my husband, life mate, father of my children, friend, and cheerleader, Dr. Kenechukwu Eneli; may our love grow sweeter, deeper, stronger, and truer, and continue to bear great fruit as the years roll by.

ABOUT THE AUTHOR

Aya Fubara Eneli is a bestselling author, certified life coach, and motivational speaker, with clients in thirteen countries. She is an alumna of The Ohio State University, where she gained her Juris Doctorate and a Master's in African/African American Studies, as well as two other degrees, and is featured in *An Encyclopedia of Pathbreaking Women at The Ohio State University*. She's been featured in a variety of media including Enterprise magazine, Black Enterprise and MSNBC.com.

Aya Eneli is passionate about family, reading, writing, and social justice. Her life purpose is to empower and equip individuals to live to their highest potential. She has been married to her husband, Dr. Kenechukwu Eneli, since 1997, and together they have five children, all of whom are entrepreneurs.

CREATING DISTINCTIVE BOOKS
WITH INTENTIONAL RESULTS

We're a collaborative group of creative masterminds with a mission to produce high-quality books to position you for monumental success in the marketplace.

Our professional team of writers, editors, designers, and marketing strategists work closely together to ensure that every detail of your book is a clear representation of the message in your writing.

Want to know more?
Write to us at info@publishyourgift.com
or call (888) 949-6228

Discover great books, exclusive offers, and more at
www.PublishYourGift.com

Connect with us on social media

@publishyourgift

CPSIA information can be obtained
at www.ICGtesting.com
Printed in the USA
FFOW04n0113160518
46680604-48774FF